I0023433

Elias F. Tanner

Genealogy of the Descendants of Thomas Tanner

of Cornwall, Connecticut, with brief notes of several allied families

Elias F. Tanner

Genealogy of the Descendants of Thomas Tanner
of Cornwall, Connecticut, with brief notes of several allied families

ISBN/EAN: 9783337101800

Printed in Europe, USA, Canada, Australia, Japan

Cover: Foto ©ninafisch / pixelio.de

More available books at **www.hansebooks.com**

THOMAS TANNER,
Of Attica.

THE GENEALOGY

OF THE DESCENDANTS OF

THOMAS TANNER, SR.

OF CORNWALL. CONNECTICUT,

WITH BRIEF NOTES OF

SEVERAL ALLIED FAMILIES

ALSO

SHORT SKETCHES OF SEVERAL TOWNS OF THEIR EARLY RESIDENCE.

A COLUMBIAN MEMORIAL

BY

REV. ELIAS F. TANNER, A. B.

"The fathers, where are they?"

(CREST, "THREE MOORS' HEADS.")

LANSING, MICH.:
DARIUS D. THORP, PRINTER AND BINDER.
1893.

DEDICATION.

To the *living descendants* of our early ancestors who braved the wilderness of a new world, endured the dangers and hardships of pioneer life, helped fight our nation's battles, defend its liberties, establish its institutions of religion and learning, promote its industries and wealth and so lay deep and broad the foundations of our nation's greatness, and into the peace, riches and blessings of whose toil and inheritance we have happily entered, this volume is affectionately inscribed by its

AUTHOR.

PREFACE.

This little work originated in a life long interest in our dear ancestors and relatives, in a desire to preserve from oblivion their honorable though humble record, and to know more of their various branches and affiliations, of their history and callings, and of their personal traits and characters. A few years since we obtained a brief outline history of our maternal ancestors and relatives, when the purpose arose of obtaining a similar paternal history. A correspondence thus begun three years ago, has developed into the present little volume. This correspondence has extended to the leading representatives of all the branches of our ancestors—perhaps fifty of them—besides an extensive correspondence with many others for correlative dates. and much reading for historic facts.

Most of our cousins and friends have cordially interested themselves in helping forward this work, without whose assistance we could not have succeeded, and to whom we take this occasion of expressing our obligation and gratitude for their help, and our pleasure in making their acquaintance. As a result of this effort, we have acquired much new knowledge of our ancestors and relatives, a better acquaintance with their times and localities, their history and con-

nection, and their labors and callings. We have
been enabled in imagination to live over again their
lives and experience back even to remote generations.
We trust this work will give our relatives a more
vivid conception of our brave and virtuous ancestors,
of their primitive times and conditions, of their
humble manner of life, and of their hardy and intelligent character; for whom we should ever cherish
a just pride, a warm love and deep reverence. And
we hope that our relatives will be stimulated to ex-
tend their correspondence and acquaintance with
their cousins, all of whom are worthy of intelligent
interest and regard, and thus become more familiar
with each other's lives, struggles and hopes.

As appropriate to the nature and object of the
work we have introduced a brief treatise on the
general subject of Genealogy, giving its definition
and stating the theoretical character of the subject
and the sources and results of investigation. We be-
lieve this will add to the value of the work and
prove instructive and interesting to our many friends
and relatives. The main body of the book we have
treated in chapters, sections, and paragraphs, thus
keeping each division and sub-division separate and
distinct. As far as possible we have carried the generations of the several lines down to the present time,
even to the babes. In a few cases we have added
probable dates to help out the imperfect record; we
have added the female and collateral lines as the
only method of making the family history complete.

In a concise way we have endeavored to make the whole work accurate, reliable and exhaustive.—The friends will observe the patriotic record of our ancestors and relatives. Not a war has been waged in defense of our country, but they have borne an honorable part. Our great grandfather was an officer in the Revolution, his sons and grandsons were in the war of 1812, and many of the later generation served in the civil war, and some laid down their lives.

Besides foot-notes of persons with whom our relatives intermarried, we have added notes in the appendix, descriptive of places where our ancestors resided and with whose scenes their lives were associated. These descriptions in the absence of full information are often imperfect, mere skeletons of scenes partially clothed and adorned.

In the course of our inquiries we have fallen upon some allied lines of Tanners, a few related families, whose lineage we have recorded in brief outline in the appendix. And we have corresponded with some of the name of whose affiliation we know nothing. Indeed, the Tanner family is becoming numerous in all parts of the country, and we are happy to learn that others are engaged in tracing their genealogy. And now, whatever the imperfections of this little work, it is the fruit of love and some sacrifice, and we trust our many friends will welcome it in the same kind spirit in which it is presented.

E. F. T.

CONTENTS.

GENERAL INTRODUCTION.

The subject of Genealogy has never been reduced to a separate science, having a well defined body of general truths or principles stated in order. However, there are some few rules which govern its treatment, as those regarding evidence of relationship and degrees of consanguinity.

Genealogy is rather a branch of history, holding an intermediate place between biography, which treats of persons, and history which treats of the rise and progress of nations. In its broader sense, genealogy covers the source and descent of large family groups, even of tribes and races of men; but in its narrower sense it is confined to the history of particular families, including their origin succession and affinities, in an ascending or descending line. It traces out and records the pedigrees of families, the names in order of the lines of descent, and the relationship of the several branches, including details of life, appearance, habits, callings and character.

Theoretical genealogy relates to the principles which govern genealogical investigation and works, and to the various and most approved methods of preserving family lineage and history.

It may trace a given family in an ascending line from

son to father up to remote ancestors. In this series the ancestors double each generation; in the first degree are two ancestors, in the second are four, in the third are eight, in the fourth sixteen, and going back to the twentieth degree, are many thousand ancestors. Or, genealogy may trace a family in a descending line, from father to son, down through many generations to the present; where the numbers are still greater; each generation increasing from three to five fold. And this is the direction in which the labors of the genealogists are now usually turned; but where the generations of descendants are many, the field is immense and the work of tracing them arduous.

Again. genealogy may trace a family in a direct line, as grandfather. father, son and grandson, or through collateral lines including its several branches and off-shoots, as uncles, aunts and cousins. These collaterals on the father's side are called *agnates*, and on the mother's side *cognates*. Ordinary genealogy includes both the main and divergent lines, arranged sometimes in a family tree, or in the form of a table, but more commonly takes the narrative form. embodying both the pedigree and the family history, births, marriages, deaths, settlement and occupation.

The methods of making records and preserving family lineage and history have been various. The pedigree and history of the privileged classes, to whom all ancient genealogies referred, were preserved in old chronicles and legends, in state records, upon family seals and rings, tablets and tombstones, monuments and mausoleums, some of which have been preserved to the present time. For many centuries the nobility and gentry took great pains to preserve the records of their descendants, because intimately connected with land tenures. But no family records of the ancient peasantry were kept; the want of surnames, of interest and intelligence, made it impracticable. In later periods and especially among christian nations, as family names were adopted and their lineage became more intelligible and as family pride and interest increased, the record of family history became more common. They are found in old letters and obituary notices, in church registers, upon family tombstones, and most frequently of all in the old family Bible. In more recent times, the state has made provision for the registration of all births, marriages and deaths.

What is the best method of family registration, and so of preserving the lineage for successive generations, has never been a subject of extensive inquiry and remains undecided. A beautiful and enduring method would be family engravings upon metal plates and tablets. A cheaper but desirable and useful method would be inscriptions upon parchment, preserved in frames or rolls. Perhaps, however, the most feasible plan, one both inexpensive and convenient is the old fashioned record in the family Bible, which is as carefully and sacredly preserved as any, and has many pleasant and hallowed associations. And certainly family pride, affection and interest dictate some form of record both permanent and beautiful, one pleasant to revive the memory of departed friends, and potent

to save trouble and secure vested rights. And modern
genealogy insists for evidence upon reliable record or
personal knowledge, and rejects hearsay and tradition.
And those records are the best, all told, which are the
most simple, intelligible, economical and permanent.
Perhaps none have more authority with the genealogist
than church registers and state records.

Practical genealogy considers the history, actual work
and results of research into ancient and modern genealogical records, and monuments, and the making of
memorials of family pedigrees and lineage.

Perhaps the most ancient genealogies are those of the
Hebrews, portions of their earlier and even later history
being little more than lineal records of families, some
of which are found in both the ascending and descending scale. And a special class was appointed to draw
up and preserve genealogical tables of the origin and
succession of families, the most complete and accurate
of those of the ancient nations. They thus preserved
the genesis and lineage of their tribal, priestly and royal
families, and the pedigree of the promised Messiah;
objects with them of the greatest moment in different
periods of their history.

Outside of this people, the earliest traces of genealogy
are found in the ancestral catalogues of the old-world
heroes. And the earliest Greek histories as well as
those of the ancient oriental nations, were mainly
genealogies, pedigrees, of their gods, heroes, priests and
princes. Also the early Roman and English histories,
aside from their war records, were largely made up of

chronicles and legends of prominent persons and events, of the names and lineage of princes and nobles, statesmen and warriors, while the pedigree of the peasant class was considered of no concern, indeed, was not practicable.

Coming down to more modern times, the earliest genealogies of our English ancestors are found about the year 1500, but were still confined to the higher classes, to the privileged families. And in the 17th century there were many genealogical books, as chronicles and legendary works, registers and necrologies, calendars and crusade rolls, which contained pedigrees or materials for them, but many of them are unreliable, made up from fictitious sources, of invented lines of ascent to some ancient and noted family.

Now prior to the 11th century family names were not found, and for two centuries later were confined to the upper classes, to princes and nobles: christian names alone being still common. But only as surnames become attached to families, can their pedigrees and lineage be easily recorded and traced. But as in later periods the middle classes rose in intelligence and influence, as family names came to be more generally adopted and family pride and interest increased, so family and parish registers of births, marriages and deaths became more practicable and common.

Now from both these higher and lower classes of old England came our New England forefathers, a mixture of aristocracy and democracy, but all lovers of civil and religious liberty. The former class composed the gentry

and clergy, men of noble and gentle blood, who held
most of the offices of church and state. And their
position, prominence and influence long remained, were
freely allowed, and were perhaps beneficial, but gradually
disappeared after the Revolution. Now with this upper
class, pride of ancestry, claims to hereditary possessions,
titles and honors, made the preservation of family
pedigrees and lineage important. And they brought
with them evidences of their lineage, armorial seals,
engraved rings, wills, deeds, and lists of names, which
being preserved, have made the tracing of their family
lineage comparatively easy. And the genealogies of
great numbers of their families have been published in
memorial volumes.

On the contrary, the middle and lower classes of
emigrants who constituted the large body of freemen,
artisans and yeomen who sought homes in the new world,
found themselves occupied in clearing away the forests,
fighting the Indians, and building and providing homes
for their families. And while men of energy, character
and thrift, and not ashamed of their worthy ancestors,
nor despising their genealogy, yet under these pressing
engagements of pioneer life, they often neglected to
make records of their family births, marriages and
deaths, and those made were often imperfect, perishable
or became difficult of access. And hence their descendants often find it impossible to discover the origin, trace
the lineage and determine the genealogy of their ancestors. And the difficulty is increased by the fact that
many families bearing the same surname, have not the

same ancestors. Many names have originated from occupation, location or some personal trait, as Painter Taylor and Tanner, Hill Dale and Waterman, White, Green and Orange, and have many distinct origins. It is a false notion that all bearing the same name, have the same original parents, or that one having the name of a noted family belongs to its stock. And this fact of distinct origins produces confusion in tracing genealogies. And the recovery of a family's pedigree thus becomes a doubtful problem, and success is often the result of accident or good fortune. Yet despite all these difficulties, the finding of old wills, deeds, chronicles, family Bibles, town and county records has enabled many to successfully trace their lineage back to remote ancestors, and to disclose the origin, succession and affinities of their families. Besides multitudes of private pedigrees and records, many hundreds of genealogies of families, many local histories with genealogical notes, dictionaries and pamphlets of genealogies, have been published, and are found in our private and state libraries. Still great multitudes of families, the large majority, and many of prominence, have no knowledge of their remote ancestors, or of their lineage and pedigree; the knowledge of few persons indeed extending back further than their grand parents.

But we have reached a period in our history, a distance from our pioneer fathers, a changed and improved condition when the historic spirit and family pride and affection should awaken an active desire to know their names, residence, affiliations and history, and to hand

2

the record down to our descendants. Our blood relation
to them and constitutional inheritance, so potent a
factor in moulding our lives should create a lively
interest in their persons and experiences, their character and conduct, and their habits and manners.   And
the more complete our knowledge of them, the better
we may understand ourselves. Such knowledge broad-
ens our sympathies with the . past generations. and
exerts an ennobling influence. It is to be hoped that
increasing numbers will engage in the laudable work of
securing a knowledge of their ancestors.

GENEALOGICAL HISTORY OF THE TANNER FAMILY.

SPECIAL INTRODUCTION.

Several traditions prevail respecting the origin of our branch of the American Tanners. The common one is that three brothers early came over from England and settled in New England. from one of whom our line has sprung. A more definite tradition says, that of three brothers in England, the oldest inheriting the property remained at home. while his two younger brothers. Thomas and William. sought their fortunes in the new world, one settling in Massachusetts and the other in Rhode Island. And early records of Tanners are found in both of these colonies.

But we suppose that the ancestors of our line, originally of West England or Wales, emigrated to Rhode Island about 1640-50, soon after the first settlement of the colony, being dissenters from the strictness of the Puritans and sympathizing with the liberal principles of Roger Williams and his companions. These English Tanners or their near descendents settled in Westerly, East and West Greenwich, Providence and Newport, Rhode Island. About a century later they began to migrate into the "up country," Connecticut and New York. where several names and lines of them are known.

CHAPTER I.

THOMAS TANNER, SR.

He is the first known ancestor and founder of the family; was born in Rhode Island about 1705-10. Married Martha ———— between 1728-30, and moved to Cornwall, Conn., in 1740, bringing considerable stock and personal property, and becoming one of the first settlers and farmers of the town. He is believed to have had four children, two sons and two daughters. but little, however, is known of his life. After enduring the hardships of the wilderness and of a pioneer life, he died in his prime in 1750, and about 45 years old. He left a young family and a widow, who in May, 1751, was appointed administrator of his estate to settle an indebtedness. His children were as follows:

Section First. WILLIAM.* born about 1729, in Rhode Island. Married Hannah Newcomb of Kent, March 23, 1749. Settled in Cornwall and had six children, Consider. Tryal. Ephraim. Ebenezer, William and Joseph.

Of his life or death little is known. See appendix for outline history of his descendants.

Section Second. MEHETABEL was born about 1733 in Rhode Island, and July 15, 1749, had a child "Sub-

---

* See Appendix A.

mit," both mother and child dying three days later, and were buried in the same grave.

Section Third. HANNAH, born about 1735, married Moses Dean of Cornwall, April 29, 1757, where she settled and had two children. I have been able to learn nothing more of her or the family.

Her children were: Ezra, born Jan. 3, 1758, and Benjamin, born Nov. 29, 1760. ·

CHAPTER II.

THOMAS TANNER, JR.

THOMAS—the fourth child of Thomas and Martha Tanner and immediate founder of our line,—was born in Cornwall on June 30, 1743, and when 18 he enlisted in the French and Indian war and served two years. He married Anna Baldwin* October 30, 1765, settled in his native town, followed the carpenter's trade, and raised a family of seven children, four sons and three daughters.

In October, 1773, a war with England pending, he was made ensign of a "trainband" of his townsmen. In May, 1776, he was appointed second lieutenant of Capt. Smith's company, Col. Bradley's battalion and Gen. Wadworth's brigade. He was in the battle of Long Island, August 27, in the retreat to New York, Harlem, Washington Heights and into Fort Washington; where, with more than 2,000 Connecticut and Maryland troops, he was taken prisoner November 16. During the night he and his comrades were marched through New York to Brooklyn, where he was held four

---

*See Appendix B.

*Anna was probably daughter of Jerjah and Mary (Ingersoll) Baldwin of Goshen, Conn., born October 1741, grand child of Richard and Ann (Oviatt) Baldwin of Milford, Conn., and great grand child of John Baldwin of same town and a descendant of a leading family of Buckinghamshire, England.

years a prisoner, meanwhile following his carpenter trade for his support. Released then on parole, he returned to his family in Cornwall, to their great joy and relief.

Soon after, in 1781, he moved with his family to New Lebanon,* New York, where some of his brother William's family had doubtless preceded him, and where he remained some twelve years, pursuing his trade, and where his two youngest children were born. In 1793 he removed to Cooperstown,† where his two oldest sons had preceded him. Here in this young thriving town he continued work at his trade till old age coming on, he died in 1817, aged 74, and was buried in the old Christ Church cemetery. His wife, Anna, followed him some four years later.

Of his moral and religious character, of his personal traits, habits and manners there is nothing known. Family tradition says he was a large, heavy man, while his wife was a quite slim and small woman; hence perhaps the medium size of most of his descendants. His army trunk, hair covered and iron bound, still exists in a great grandson's family at South Cortland, N. Y.

* See Appendix C.   † See Appendix D.

CHAPTER III.

IRA TANNER. SR.

IRA—first son of Thomas Tanner, was born June 12. 1767, in Cornwall where he spent his youth amid the rude pioneer scenes and conditions of a new country. and under the trials and excitement of the American Revolution. In 1781 he moved with his parents to New Lebanon and thence, in 1789, when 22. to Cooperstown. Early in 1790, at Pierstown, he married Julia Fitch* of Plainfield, and after a year or two, settled on a farm on "Tanner Hill" in Otsego and had eleven children, four sons and seven daughters. His wife dying in 1809, he married again in 1810. Rhoda Hubbard of Pierstown,† by whom he had two sons.

In the early summer of 1844, himself and wife visited their daughter Mrs. Phebe Stewart in Herman, St. Law-

---

* Julia was daughter of Elias Fitch, native of Lebanon, Connecticut, and of English origin, who settled on land in Plainfield about 1790, and who died between 1820-25, age 75. She was the oldest of six brothers and sisters, Augustia, Elias P., Charles, George, and C. Augustus; was born between 1768-70 and died in 1809, age 40.

†Pierstown, some three miles north-west of Cooperstown was simply an early settlement of emigrants from Connecticut and Massachusetts, prominent among whom was the Piers family, consisting of six brothers who took up large tracts of land. During the first decade, the settlers were as numerous as those of the village; saw and grist mills, taverns, stores, shops and dwellings were erected, and a flourishing business carried on. But, save farming, all those early interests have long since disappeared.

rence County, New York, where both sickened and died
of malarial fever, the former June 13, age 79 the latter
June 11, age 64, and were buried in East Dekalb in the
same grave.

Ira Tanner was a man of medium height, fair complexion, blue eyes and dark hair. He was a farmer in
moderate circumstances, and for forty years "town con-
stable;" a man of active temperament, of warm social
habits, and of some local prominence, but not of
decided moral and religious character.

Section First. PHEBE—oldest child of Ira Tanner,
was born in January, 1791, in Cooperstown, but spent
her youth on the farm, and received a common school
education. She married Philomon Stewart,* carpenter,
May 21, 1809, and the same year moved to DeKalb,† St.
Lawrence county, where for sixteen years Mr. Stewart
followed his trade. In 1825 they settled on a farm in
Herman, where they raised their six children, passed
the balance of their days in useful industry, and died
both the same year, Philemon in June, 1871, aged 83,
and Phebe in July 13, aged 80.

They were both of social habits, afforded their friends
a generous hospitality, were professing and practical
Christians, and their memory will long remain blessed.
Their children were as follows:

1st. IRA, born in 1811, in DeKalb, married Adaline

---

* Mr. Stewart was a native of Williamstown, Mass., where he was
born in 1788, and where are graves of his ancestors, and near which
place, in N. Adams, were relatives living in 1858.

† See Appendix E.

Barber,* of Canton, December 3, 1840, and settled on a small place near his father. He had by his wife twelve children, and after spending an industrious though impecunious life, was shot by an insane son February 14, 1879, aged 68. He was a great fox hunter and story teller.

His children were: 1st, ELLEN, who married Charles Clark and settled in Waddington; 2d, HENRY, who served in the civil war and died of wounds received in battle; 3d, ANN, who is insane in some asylum; 4th, GEORGE, who served in the army, was wounded and became insane; 5th, STERLING, who died young; 6th, JANE, who is insane in the county house; 7th, MILTON, also insane in Ovid Asylum; 8th, PHEBE, resident of Hermon; 9th, ADDIE, who married Elmer Smith and settled in Russell; 10th, ARDELIA, who married Samuel Cotton, and dwells in Hermon; 11th, SOPHRONIA, who died in infancy; 12th, SOPHRONIA, 2d, who is living in Hermon.

2d. JULIA, born in 1813, in DeKalb, married Abijah Little and settled in Canton on a farm. She had one child and died in 1884, age 71.

Her child, EURETTA, born about 1834, married Alvin Barber of Canton and had three children, LAVINA and LILLIAN, both married, and GIDEON, who is unmarried.

3d. JARVIS, born June 4, 1818, in DeKalb, married Harriet Tamblin July 27, 1852, and settled on the

* Adaline Stewart is still living in 1892, has been subject most of her life to constitutional insanity, which she inherited from her mother, and which she has handed down to several of her children.

paternal homestead. He had two children and died after a quiet and useful life, March 27, 1887, age 69.*

His children were: 1st, MARIA, born September 15, 1853, married first; R. Maxon and had one son, ELMER S., and married again, L. Powell and settled in the old home: 2d, DWIGHT. born July 23, 1858, who became a farmer and remains unmarried.

4th. ANGELINE, born in 1820, in DeKalb: married Henry Mattoon in 1844, settled in Armourdale, Kansas, —a suburb of Kansas City,—where she is still living, a widow, and her three children.

Her children are: 1st, ESTHER born in 1846, married Henry Marshall and settled in Kansas City; 2d, EUGENE born in 1848, married and settled near his mother; 3d, George born in 1850. married. and lives in New Mexico.

5th. ADALINE. born in March, 1824, in DeKalb: married Rufus B. Clarke in December, 1843, and settled West and died May, 1846, aged 22.

Her child, ADALINE E., was born in November, 1845; married first, T. C. McLaughlin, physician, of Dubuque, Iowa, July, 1865, and had three children; married second, R. B. Conover, of Pasadena, Cal., January 1, 1875.

Her children were: 1st, ALICE A., born in September, 1867, and died in infancy: 2d, NELLIE M., born in September, 1868, married James F. Roof September 15, 1892; 3d, THOMAS C., JR., born in 1872, and died in infancy.

6th. AURILLA, born in 1828. in Hermon; married

*His wife, Harriet, who died two-and-a-half years later, will long be remembered as a very plain, but most excellent and charitable woman.

Morse Baird in 1850 and settled in Hermon; had three children and died in 1871, aged 43.

Her children were: 1st, LILLIAN, born about 1851, married John Neath, settled in Pennsylvania and has seven children; 2d, KATE, born about 1853, married Jason Kinney, lived in Liverpool, N. Y., had five children and died in 1886, aged 33; 3d, MERTON, born about 1855, lives in Gouverneur, N. Y., and is unmarried.

Section Second. JULIA—second child of Ira Tanner, was born in March 1793, in Otsego, raised on the farm, married John Williams* of Pierstown, May 10, 1810, and settled in Cooperstown. She had one child and soon died, September 22, 1812, leaving her husband and young child, at the age of 19.

Her descendant, JULIUS WM., born April 18, 1812, in Cooperstown, married Lucy Ann Webb October 28, 1833, settled near home, had two children and is supposed to be dead.

His children were: 1st, MARIETTA, born June 24, 1837, married E. B. Stephens, of Pierstown in 1859, and settled in Binghampton, has two children. NINA LOUISA born August 20, 1862, and GRACE W., born January 7, 1867. 2d, JOHN E., born October 10, 1841, married 1st, Carrie N. Ostrander, in 1865, and had one child, married 2d, Eva M. Bailey November 26, 1890,

---

*John was the son of John Williams, Sr., and grandson of Isaac Williams, who emigrated with his parents from Goshen, Connecticut in 1793 to Pierstown. He was the third of six brothers, Isaac, Jr., Ozias, Lee, Joseph and Stephen, who became prominent men and their descendants numerous. John was born between 1785-90, married three times, followed farming, and died aged 80.

and settled in Des Moines, Iowa. His child CARRIE M.,
born February 19, 1866, married Morith Holbrook in
1888.

Section Third. OLIVIA—third child of Ira Tanner,
was born November 15, 1794, in Otsego, where she received her early training and education. She married
Ethan Beach* of Plainfield, Otsego County, in 1816,
moved to and settled in Hamilton, Madison County, on a
farm, where all her nine children were born. Having
raised her family, she died in 1877, age 83.

She was a woman of decided character, of christian
principles, a faithful wife and good mother.

Outline history of her children.

1st. MELLISSA, born May 24. 1818, married Masan
H. Cushman December 28, 1846, settled in Silver
Creek, had four children and died April 25, 1891,
aged 73.

Her children were: 1st, MASAN E., born October 28.
1848, married Adelaide McDaniels, farmer, March 11.
1879, has one child, GEORGE E., and is settled in Silver
Creek; 2d, JOSHUA E., born April 12, 1851, married
Millie E. Young November 28, 1874, farmer, and has
two children, VERA C. and LIVIA E.; 3d, MAROE,
born September 28, 1856, died at 4 years of age; 4th.
LIVIA, born November 26, 1860, married Willis B.
Horton June 4, 1880, farmer, and has no children.

2d. E. ORLANDO. born June 28, 1820, married Ros-

---

*Ethan Beach was a native of New Lebanon, where his parents who
were of New England stock, early settled. He was born about 1793,
and in youth moved with his father's family to Plainfield, was an
excellent man, died 1874.

ina Holmes of Hamilton, March 8, 1847, settled at South Dayton, had five children and was killed by a falling tree.

His children, MILLARD, MADELLON, EDWIN, WILLIAM, NELLIE, all married and had children, except the oldest. Madellan and William are deceased.

3d. LUCY ANN, born May 27, 1823, married Hiram Weller of Hamilton, September 17, 1840, settled in same town, had seven children and died of blood poison in December 1878, age 55.

Her children are: EMILY, FLORA, LEONORA, CHARLES, FRANK, MARY and HIRAM; are all living and married and all have children except the three oldest.

4th. HIRAM P., born May 14, 1825, married Martha Slaughter of Southern Ohio in 1858, where he settled and had one son, LEE. His wife dying soon, he married again Elizabeth Harpole of same place, by whom he had ten children, settled last in Cornwallis, Oregon, and died March, 1890.

His children are: CHARLES, CLYDE, MARY, ELLA, JOHN, MINNIE, LIZZIE, EMMA, and two who are deceased. All the others are living with their mother in Oregon. Lee is married, settled in Cornwallis and has one child.

5th. SYLVESTER H., born April 6, 1827. Married Lucy Brooks of Chenango County, June 27, 1849, settled in South Dayton, and had four children. His wife dying, he married again, Polly Doane, by whom he had one child and died in 1872, of consumption.

His children were: DERMORIT and LaMOTT both of whom married and have had children, CALPHURNIA who died in August 1890, ETHAN and MERTON.

6th. L. MERTON, born May 16, 1829, married Adelia Nash, of Hamilton, in October, 1854, settled in Poolville, had four children. and is still living.

His children are all deceased save one, ARTHUR, born about 1865, and married in 1886 and settled on his father's farm.

7th. CALPHURNIA, born in July 1831; married Damon Richmond of Poolville, February 6, 1861, where she settled: had one child and is still living, a widow since 1883.

Her child, MARY, born September 25, 1866, married S. W. Berry in 1887, and has one child HENRY.

8th. G. EDWARDS born October 14, 1833, married Emma C. Walker of Goshen, December 16, 1869, and settled on the old homestead, has two children and still living.

His children are: B. WALKER and JENNIE L. neither of whom are married.

9th. MADELLON E., born August 9, 1837, married Arton P. Ford of Otselic, in the spring of 1865, settled in Deposit, Broome County, had one child and died in September, 1887.

Her child is A. MERTON, unmarried and living in De Ruyter, Madison County.

Section Fourth. FITCH—fourth child and oldest son of Ira Tanner—was born April 24, 1796, in Otsego, received a limited education, was raised a farmer, and

lived several years with his uncle, Elias P. Fitch of
Plainfield. In 1814 he was drafted into the army of
the "war of 1812," and served six months at Sackett's
Harbor. Between 1817-20, he moved to DeKalb, married Lora Dewey of the same town March 11, 1824, and
settled on a farm. He was unfortunate in business and
April 15, 1827, buried his wife; she leaving one child,
ELIAS, who died in 1830, age 5. He married again,
Divine G. Eager* of Gouverneur, September 15, 1829,
and settled again in his adopted town. In 1834, he
moved to Gouverneur and worked a farm eleven years,
when being unfortunate and health failing, he returned to
DeKalb. After suffering many years from heart disease,
he suddenly dropped dead in the woods April 16, 1855,
age 59, and was buried in East DeKalb. He left a
wife and three children.

Fitch Tanner had sandy hair, blue eyes and light
complexion, was of medium height and well built, was
fond of reading, of quiet and industrious habits, of upright principles and christian character and professions.
He left his children no worldly goods, but bequeathed
to them a good name and a pleasant memory. His
children were:

---

*Divine was daughter of James and Anne Eager of Warwick, Massa-
chusetts. She was the third child of seven brothers and sisters, was
born October 21, 1796, "brot up" with her aunt, Divine Conant, in Win-
chester, New Hampshire, and learned "the man-tailors' trade" which
she followed many years. About 1824, she moved "over the mountains"
to Gouverneur, New York, married in 1829, became a widow in 1855 and
died September 20, 1888, age 92, and was buried in East DeKalb. She had
black eyes and hair, a warm temperament and great energy, was a
faithful wife, a loving mother, and for many years a professing
christian.

3

1st. ELIAS, born October 21, 1833, in DeKalb, was educated in the common schools, at Williams College, and Union Theological Seminary, married Maria Beckwith* of Barrington, Massachussets, April 29, 1863, settled in Wisconsin and then in Michigan, labored 21 years in the Presbyterian ministry and nine years at farming, has six children and lost one.

His children are: 1st, J. EDITH born June 5, 1864 in Barton, Wisconsin, educated at Olivet College, Michigan, married Edwin W. Sprague of St. Joseph, August 12, 1888, and settled in Chicago; 2d, S. AGNES, born November 20, 1866, in Pardeeville, Wisconsin, educated at Olivet College, teacher, unmarried; 3d, HARRY B., born September 16, 1868, in Grand Ledge, Michigan, farmer, unmarried; 4th, ALBERT F., born January 14, 1870, in Grand Ledge, farmer, unmarried; 5th, MARY E., born December 15, 1871, in La Salle, Michigan, type writer in Chicago; 6th, Lora D., born December 30, 1873, in California, Michigan, student; 8th, FERDIE, born February 27, 1876, died in infancy.

2d. LORA A., born August 14, 1835, in Gouverneur, married George Bryte, of Prairie City, Ill., March 5, 1865, and settled in same town, has two children, and is still living. Her children are: 1st, ELIAS T., born May 20, 1867, married Ettie Keyser September 28, 1892, and settled in Farragut, Ia., farmer; 2d, EDITH J., born

---

* Maria was daughter of Barzillai and Mercy Beckwith, native of Barrington and descendant of the Beckwith's of Lyme, Connecticut. She was born January 13, 1833, and the third child of six brothers and sisters.

October 20, 1873, in Prairie City, educated in high school, teacher, unmarried.

3d. JULIA, born May 12, 1837, in Gouverneur, settled in DeKalb, cared many years for her aged mother, and remains unmarried.

Section Fifth. CATHARINE—fifth child of Ira Tanner, was born January 9, 1798, in Otsego, where she obtained her early education, moved to DeKalb in 1809, married John Westcott* July, 1816, settled on a farm in the same town, and had fifteen children there, twelve of whom grew to man and womanhood. Having served her day and generation, she died July 5, 1865, aged 68. She was of quiet and sedate habits, but of great energy and industry, a faithful wife, a good mother and an earnest consistent Christian, in communion with the Methodist church. Her children were as follows:

1st. ALVIN WESTCOTT, born June 15, 1817, married Margaret Brooks of Russell, May 1, 1850, settled as farmer in DeKalb, and had three children. His wife dying he married again, Nancy Anderson of same town, April 29, 1858, and had two children. He moved to Trowbridge, Michigan in 1868, and died February 27, 1881, age 67.

His children were: 1st, MARY, born in DeKalb, July 5, 1851, married James McCullough, of Lisbon,

---

*John Westcott, a native of Rhode Island, was born October 6, 1786, and one of ten children, Warner, Samuel, Davis, Daniel, Nellie, Sally, Annie, Dorcas and Mercy. He early moved to Cooperstown, and thence in 1809, with a company of Tanners, to DeKalb; followed farming and carpentry, and after an active and upright life, died October 9, 1865, aged 79.

and settled on a farm, had five children, and moved thence in 1879 to Hammond, Wisconsin. Her children were: CHARLES L., born August 2, 1869, died in infancy; GEORGE H. born August 20, 1870; FRANK A. born September 13, 1874; HOWARD J., born October 4, 1877, and died in May 1892, and a daughter born August 4, 1879 and died in infancy. 2d. LAURA, born in DeKalb January 25, 1853, married Rollin Wood of Trowbridge, Michigan, settled on a farm and has four children. 3d. LUCY, born in DeKalb, March 13, 1857, married George McCullough of Hammond, Wisconsin, June 3, 1880, and has five children, JOHN V., born October 11, 1881; FLOYD L., born September 15, 1882; ADDIE M., born July 30, 1886; ALLEN J., born November 6th, 1888; IVA D., born February 28, 1890. 4th. CLARA, born in DeKalb March 7, 1859, married Abel Russon, of Trowbridge, March 30, 1881, settled on a farm and has one child, MABEL E., born October, 1892. 5th. MARCIA, born in DeKalb January 29, 1862, married William H. Thompson, farmer, of Trowbridge, October 7, 1882, and has three children.

2d. HENRY WESTCOTT, born September 10, 1818, married Ellen Rogerson, of E. Bloomfield, July 3, 1848, settled in Manchester on a farm, has two children and is living: 1st, ORLIN, born in East Bloomfield, July 20, 1849, and remains unmarried; 2d, LYMAN, born January 11, 1856, in E. Bloomfield, is unmarried, and painter by trade.

3d. ORVIL WESTCOTT, born December 3, 1819, married Sarah Scott, of Gates, February 3, 1847, settled in

Rochester till 1854, when he moved to Ottawa, Ill., was whip manufacturer, had six children and died June 14, 1888.

His children were as follows: 1st, MILTON S., born June 2, 1849, in Rochester; married Mary Walters, of Ottawa, where he settled and has seven children; 2d, MYRON B., born in Rochester November 5, 1850, died in Ottawa, unmarried, September 23, 1877; 3d, EDWIN E., born in Rochester October 31, 1853, married Ella P. Martin, of Ottawa, April 29, 1878, where he settled and follows painting, and has three children; 4th, EMMA, twin, born October 31, 1853, married Alonzo Hinchey, of Briston, Mich., May 26, 1879, where she settled, and has no issue; 5th, LELAND D., born in Ottawa May 12, 1864, and died in infancy; 6th, LELA, twin, born May 12, 1864, married Christopher Stewart, of Ottawa, May 22, 1880, settled in same place and has six children.

4th. CLARISSA WESTCOTT, born May 22, 1821, married Charles Rundell, of DeKalb, March 3, 1843, settled in Russell, had no children, buried her husband, and died after many years of suffering August 3, 1889, aged 68.

5th. MARIA WESTCOTT, born August 19, 1822, followed cheese making many years, never married, and now lives with her brother John in DeKalb.

6th. ANDREW J. WESTCOTT, born November 3, 1824, married Celia A. Burnett, of DeKalb, February 22, 1853, and followed shoemaking. In 1867 he moved to River Falls, Wis., had four children, and died March 26, 1885, aged 61.

His children are: 1st, IDA, born in DeKalb February 4, 1857, married February 28, 1884, J. Monroe Bushnell of Wyocena, Wis., where she settled and has no issue; 2d, ELSWORTH, born in DeKalb, March 3, 1865, and remains unmarried; 3d, MAUD, born in Elsworth, Wis., May 14, 1871, married Hamilton H. Watson, farmer, May 10, 1892, and settled in Poynette, Wis.; 4th, another child, name not known.

7th. HIRAM WESTCOTT, born March 2, 1826, died August 18, 1828.

8th. JOHN W. WESTCOTT, born April 25, 1827, married Frances Hemenway January 14, 1850, of DeKalb, where he first settled and followed dairying, then moved to Russell in 1860 on to a farm of his own, and then back to DeKalb in 1872, becoming meanwhile a successful and wealthy farmer.

He is still living, and had three children, as follows: 1st, EFFIE, born in DeKalb June 7, 1857, married A. B. Cole of Canton, physician, June 28, 1875, moved to Fergus Falls, Minn., in 1882, and has no issue; 2d, INA N., born in Russell April 14, 1864, and died in infancy; 3d, JOHN F., born in Russell November 1, 1871, and died in infancy.

9th. EMILY WESTCOTT, born October 5, 1830, married Erwin W. Halligas January 1, 1856, settled in DeKalb on a farm, and has two sons, as follows: 1st, CHARLES A., born August 22, 1859, remains single and follows bee-keeping; 2d, ELMER E., born June 30, 1871, married January 20, 1891, Hattie Crane of Rensselaer Falls, where he is settled on a farm and has one child, LAURA E., born November 22, 1892.

10th. ORIS WESTCOTT, born May 29, 1832, married Catharine McGruer in January, 1858, settled in DeKalb on a farm, had two children, and died July 4, 1881, aged 59. He was an industrious farmer, an excellent citizen, a staunch temperance man, held offices of trust, and his death was much lamented.

His children are: 1st, FRANK J., born in Russell October 12, 1858, is unmarried, followed farming, then mining, and is now salesman in Park City, Utah; 2d, FLORA S., born in DeKalb June 23, 1874, and lives with her mother, unmarried, in Ogdensburg.

11th. DAVIS WESTCOTT, born August 26, 1833, married Betsey Brooks of DeKalb January 5, 1857, settled in Trowbridge on a farm and had one child. His wife dying in 1884, he married again, Eveline Firth, November 24, 1885. His son, ROLLIN E., born March 4, 1868, married Barbara Jewson April 7, 1892, and settled in Trowbridge.

12th. FRANCIS WESTCOTT, born October 13, 1835, married Susan E. Ferguson of Meridian, Minn., September 26, 1865, settled in Wilton on a farm, had three children, and died January 29, 1892. He served in the civil war and was wounded. He was a member of the Methodist church, an earnest temperance man, an upright citizen and much beloved.

His children were: 1st, CLARA B., born June 26, 1866, married Chas. H. Austin of Marshall, Minnesota, January 29, 1891, and has one child, VINIE E.; 2d CORA E., born January 15, 1868, married E. W. Ward of Marshall, July 21, 1887, and had one son, ROY F.,

born in 1890 and died in infancy; 3d, ABBIE E., born
June 25, 1871, married E. P. Walker November 7,
1889 and had two children, VERNIE, born in 1890, and
LOYD F., born in 1892.

13th. HORACE WESTCOTT, born March 8, 1837,
married Macy Mouthorp of KeKalb, January 16, 1862,
settled in Canada till 1869 and then on a farm in
Russell and had two children, 1st, ELMER born September 4, 1863, and died July 18, 1885, age 22; 2d,
ELLA, born July 15, 1867, and lives unmarried with
her parents.

14th. MILTON WESTCOTT, born July 31, 1838, and
died in infancy.

15th. FRANKLIN WESTCOTT, born February 25,
1840, and died young, September 11, 1851, age 11. Up
to present date Catherine T. Westcott has over 80 descendants.

Section Sixth. CLARISSA—sixth child of Ira Tanner—was born in July 1799, in Otsego, where she received
her early training and education. Between 1815-20
she went to DeKalb and married Hubbard Dewey* of
the same town in 1823, where she settled, had two
children and was left a widow in 1826. Returning to

---

*Hubbard was son of Hon. Joshua Dewey and Lora Loomis, natives of
Lebanon, Connecticut, who settled in Cooperstown in 1791. He taught
there the first school, and was the first assembly man from Otsego county.
In 1809 he moved with his family to DeKalb, thence to to Sackett's Harbor where he buried his wife, thence to Brooklyn, and died with his
daughter Emeline, in Watertown, in 1864, age 97. Hubbard, born about
1796, and deceased in 1826, was one of 10 children, Chester, Belden,
Lucius, Eliza, Louisa, Lora, Marcia, Emeline and Lewis, who alone is
now living in Brooklyn.

Otsego, she married again, Jesse S. Burgess,* December 21, 1834, settled in Richfield Springs, had two sons, and died April 18, 1871, aged 72, her husband dying three months later. She lived in moderate circumstances, was a hard working woman, a faithful wife and good mother.

Her children were as follows:

1st. ELIZA DEWEY, born May 25, 1825, in DeKalb, married Cyrus Williamson March 30, 1851, settled in Warren on a farm, had four children, and is now living a widow with her son.

Her children are: 1st, EMILY, born March 30,1852, and died May 30, 1863, aged 11; 2d,. VIOLETTA, born March 18, 1854, married James Hopkinson December 13, 1871, settled in Warren, and has one child, EMMA, born in 1874; 3d, NORMAN J., born April 5, 1856, married Louisa Edgett January 16, 1879, and settled in Warren on the "old farm," and has two children: MABLE, born in 1881, and BESSIE L., born in 1885; 4th, HATTIE E., born January 13, 1858, and lives unmarried in Warren with her mother.

2d. LOUISA DEWEY, born January 21, 1827, married Russell Beadle November 24, 1850, settled in Otsego county, had three sons, and buried her husband in 1862. She married again David Lewis, was left again a widow in 1888, and is still living with her children in Fly Creek.

---

* Jessie S. was son of John Burgess of Plainfield, Conn., a descendant of the Burgesses of England, the name coming from the "House of Burgesses" The ancestors early emigrated to New England, where they became numerous and highly respected. Jesse S. was born in 1789, and died July 19, 1871, aged 82.

Her children are: 1st, ALBERT K., born December 10, 1842, married Delia M. Hanretty October 6, 1879, and has five children: FRED A., RUSSELL A., FLORENCE L., ARTHUR W. and BLANCH E.; 2d, HORACE A., born November 17, 1856, married Jennie M. Fearn February 20, 1884, settled in Fly Creek, and has one child, MABEL M.; 3d, CHARLES W., born October 7, 1858, married Carrie R. Loomis October 28, 1891, and settled in Richfield Springs.

3d. J. WHEATON BURGESS, born April 21, 1836. He went to Providence, Rhode Island, and engaged in manufacture. Is supposed to have married and settled there, but of him or his family nothing is known.

4th. JOHN H. BURGESS, born March 4, 1839, married Emeline C. Main December 12, 1867, had two children, was left a widower in 1879, and married again Mary L. Lewis, December 17, 1881. He served three years in the civil war, bears six honorable wounds, and has since followed school teaching.

His children are: 1st, CARRIE E., born November 12, 1869, and married Wm. Hatch, March 13, 1889, of Columbia, New York; 2d, JESSIE M. born June 27, 1873, and is unmarried.

Section Seventh. MARIA—seventh child of Ira Tanner—was born in Otsego, March 3, 1801, married Russell Bourn October 23, 1823, settled in Fly Creek on a farm, where she had five children, and where, after a useful and Christian life, she died November 14, 1849, aged 48.

Her children are as follows:

1st. JULIA, born September 17, 1824, and died, unmarried, February 9, 1843, aged 19.

2d. ORLANDO, born April 19, 1828, married H. Jane Chamberlain May, 1857, settled in Otsego as a farmer, had one child, and buried his wife in 1880. He is now living with his daughter.

His child: FLORA B., born February 7, 1870, married Henry Chapin February 23, 1887, settled in Fly Creek, and has three children still living.

Her children are: 1st, LULA, born August 13, 1887; 2d, BESSIE, born March 31, 1889; 3d, CLAUD, born October 31, 1891.

3d. MENZO, born October 15, 1833, married Elvira Pierce February 7, 1856, settled in Fly Creek as a farmer, has two children, and is still living.

His children are: 1st, MENZO E., born November 21, 1856, married Cora E. Veber September 15, 1879, settled near home, had one child, and buried his wife. He married again Mrs. E. Williams and settled in the town of Maryland. His child, FLORA E., was born in 1884; 2d, ELLA M., born February 11, 1866, married Lewis Mann September 20, 1882, settled in Fly Creek, and has no children.

4th. LUNA M., born July 2, 1837, married Thomas Chamberlain July 1, 1858, settled on a farm in Fly Creek, has three children, and is still living.

Her children are: 1st, CHARLES F., born March 4, 1860, married Sarrie C. Walrath December 15, 1880, settled in Pierstown, has one child, MAUD M., born

August 20, 1882; 2d, FRANK R., born September 1, 1862, married Juvie House January 12, 1887, settled in Schuyler Lake on a farm; 3d, CARRIE M., born December 9, 1874, is unmarried.

5th. RUSSELL T., born May 14, 1847, is unmarried. Living in Cooperstown, his occupation is the care of an invalid for the last ten years.

Section Eighth. ZERA—eighth child of Ira Tanner—was born in 1803 on "Tanner Hill," Otsego, spent his early life on his father's farm, married in 1825 Lucy Chapman,* and settled in his native town eleven years, and had four children. About 1836 he moved with his family to South Cortland, took up land, followed farming, and resided there the balance of his life. Here he had five more children, and died suddenly of heart disease while sitting in his wagon September 5, 1864, aged 61. He was a successful business man, became quite wealthy, was a respected citizen, a kind father, a moral and religious man, and a member of the Christian church.

His children were:

1st. LAURA, born in 1826 in Otsego, married three times, had no children, and died November 14, 1889, aged 63.

2d. CATHARINE, born March 8, 1828, and died in infancy.

3d. MARTHA, born July 19, 1830, in Otsego, mar-

---

* Lucy Chapman was a native of Pierstown and daughter of Chauncey N. Chapman, a soldier in the war of 1812. Lucy died August 29, 1892, aged 84.

ried Riley Niles in 1852, settled in South Cortland on a farm, had four children, and is still living.

Her children are: 1st, DEWITT, born in 1856, and living in Wayne county; 2d, MILLARD, born in 1859, living near home; 3d, IRA, born in 1862, married and settled in Denver, Col.; 4th, a daughter deceased.

4th. MARIA, born November 22, 1832, in Otsego, married first Thomas Ford about 1855, who served in the civil war and was killed. She married second B. F. Brooks in 1865, had two children, and is living.

Her children are: 1st, ZERA FORD, born in 1857, his marriage and settlement not known; 2d, LOUISA BROOKS, born in 1866, and living in Tioga Center.

5th. MARY, born December 7, 1835 in Otsego, died young at 5 years.

6th. JULIA, born November 14, 1837, in South Cortland, married first George Laundsbury in 1856, and settled in Cortland, had two children and buried her husband. She married second Samuel Burdick about 1870, settled at Blodgett's Mills, had one child and died after a long sickness, October 5, 1891, age 54.

Her children were: 1st, FRED LAUNDSBURY, born in 1857, living in Cortland; 2d, GEORGE LAUNDSBURY born about 1859, and living in New York City; 3d, DELLA BURDICK, born in 1871, and living in Blodgett's Mills.

7th. AMANDA, born October 12, 1840, in South Cortland, married Charles Sanders about 1862-4, settled in Cortland, had four children and is still living.

Her children are: 1st, LULA, born in 1866, married a Mr. Northrup and settled in Syracuse; 2d, CARRIE, born in 1870, life unknown; 3d, CHARLEY, born in 1874, and unmarried; 4th, a son, deceased.

8th. ZERA, born March 31, 1842, in South Cortland, married Ella Lacy in 1876, settled on the old homestead, had three children, and is still living. His children were: 1st, RAY, born in 1877; 2d, ETHAN B., born in 1881; 3d, a son, deceased.

9th. ARVILLA, born October 5, 1844, in South Cortland, married E. M. Thompson in 1865, and settled in Waverly, has three children, and is still living. Her children are: 1st, EDWIN, born in 1866, history unknown; 2d, ELLA, born in 1872, married a Mr. Williams, settlement not known; 3d, LUCY, born in 1880, history unknown.

Section Ninth. EUNICE — ninth child of Ira Tan - ner—was born August 12, 1804, in Otsego, received here her early training, married at the old homestead Hiram Main,* a Baptist minister, October 22, 1828, settled for short periods in various towns of the state, had nine children, three sons and six daughters, and died suddenly of heart disease at Antwerp, June 2, 1866, aged 62, and was buried in Russell.

Eunice possessed a cheerful and social nature, spent a life of toilsome and Christian usefulness, and was a faithful wife and good mother.

Her children were as follows:

1st. ROSWELL P., born in Springfield July 20, 1829,

---

* Hiram, son of Joseph Main of Stonington, Conn., was born in 1806, one of eleven children, six sons and five daughters. He died in 1878 in Russell.

married Maria Drake June 14, 1854, settled first in Antwerp and last in Canton, followed the tinner's trade, had one child, and died suddenly of heart disease in the Adirondacks July 20, 1882, aged just 53.

His child: IDA MAY, born in March, 1855, married John Russell of Canton and settled in Sacramento, Cal. She has two children, JOSIE and JOHN.

2d. JULIA M., born June 28, 1831, in Otsego, married Eleazer Carr of Russell July 2, 1854, settled in the same village, has three children, and is still living.

Her children were: 1st, FLORA, born in March, 1857, married Charles Shaw, settled in Russell, and has five children: BERTIE S., WILLIE E., BLANCH L., CLAUD D. and JENNIE L.; 2d, CLARA C., born in August, 1859, married F. C. Crawford, settled in Wexford, Mich., and has four children: GERTIE L., FLORA M., MARION and MAY, twins; 3d, JENNIE M., born in August, 1861, married Lucius Lamphear, and settled in Carthage, N. Y.

3d. ELIZA MATILDA, born in May, 1833, in Otsego, married: 1st, Martin Tripp, January 20, 1850; 2d, William Hamilton, September 14, 1876, major in the civil war; 3d, Martin Rugg, June 28, 1888, settled in Carthage, has no children, and lives in affluent circumstances.

4th. IRA H., born December 6, 1834, in Burlington, married Nancy King April 14, 1860, settled in Russell, follows carpenters' trade, has two children, and is still living.

His children are: 1st, GEORGE, born in August, 1863,

married Florence Howard, and settled in Chateaugay; 2d, IDA KING, adopted, born in January, 1856, married William Hosford, settled near Russell, has two sons: JOHN, deceased, and WILLIE.

5th. MARY JANE, born in Norwich November 24, 1836; died in infancy, aged 1 year.

6th. MARTHA L., born in Burlington August 19, 1838, married Charles Brown, September 16, 1866, settled in Antwerp on a farm, and has three children: 1st, MYRON, born June 1, 1866, unmarried and at home; 2d, MAY L., born May 7, 1870, married Leo Hogan, and settled in Antwerp; 3d, MERTON, born September 12, 1873, unmarried, and is a cheesemaker.

7th. EMELINE C., born May 19, 1840, in Otsego, married John H. Burgess December 12, 1867, settled in Richfield Springs, had two children, and died July 24, 1879, aged 39.

Her children are: 1st, CARRIE E., born November 12, 1869; 2d, JESSE M., born June 27, 1873.

8th. CAROLINE A., born July 9, 1843, in Charlotteville, married Smith Chase February 5, 1861, settled in Russell, had one son, and died September 8, 1867, aged 24.

Her son, GLEN, born January, 1861, married Anderson. He lives in Kansas, and travels with a theatrical troupe.

9th. JOSEPH H., born in 1845, died between 1847-8 in young childhood.

Section Tenth. LATHROP — tenth child of Ira Tanner—was born in Otsego in 1805, and raised on the farm. When a young man he buried his bride, and remained ever after unmarried. He followed farming, day labor, hunting and fishing, and was especially fond of his gun. He followed a singular and irregular manner of life. After 1856 he lived with his sister, Mrs. Phebe Stewart in Hermon, and later with his nephew, Jarvis Stewart, in the same home. He died impecunious, in 1885, aged 80, and was buried at East DeKalb.

Section Eleventh. PEABODY — eleventh child of Ira Tanner—was born September 26, 1808, in Otsego. From the age of 17-21, he lived in Plainfield with his uncle, Elias P. Fitch, married Roxanna Farrar in Otsego December 16, 1830, where he settled on a farm. Had here five children, two of them dying young. In 1851 he moved with his family to Chautauqua county, and thence, in 1856, to Evans, Erie county, where he settled again on a farm. After twenty-two years of successful business, he suddenly died of heart disease while sitting in his chair November 6, 1878, aged 70, leaving a wife still living and four children. He was a man of medium stature and dark curly hair, of industrious and social habits, and of Christian character and profession.

His children were as follows:

1st. MARY ANN, born in 1832 in Otsego, and died young in 1839, aged 7.

2d. HANNAH, born in 1834, and died the same date as her older sister, aged 5.

3d. MELLISSA, born July 29, 1836, in Otsego, moved with her parents to Western New York, married

4

George Wilcox of Evans January 1, 1857, settled in
Angola, had six children, and died of bronchitis September 4, 1890, aged 54.

Her children are: 1st, FRANK A., born November 22,
1858, married Sophie Arner April 10, 1880, had one
child, and mother and child dying June 2, 1884, he
married again Belle Crissey June 23, 1889; 2d, EVERETT
L., born June 24, 1861, married Bertha Schlender June
21, 1883, and has two children: ALICE M., born May 23,
1·86, and GRACE E., born September 14, 1890; 3d,
MURTON O., born March 7, 1863, and died unmarried,
January 31, 1882, aged 19, from gunshot wound received
while hunting; 4th, ALICE R., born June 11, 1866, married David E. Smith September 23, 1888, settled in
Angola, and has one child, MARABEL, born July 29,
1889; 5th, MARY M., born January 9, 1870, married
Arthur R. Carr September 23, 1888, and has one child,
HARRIET M., born May 5, 1891; 6th, ELSIE L., born
June 15, 1873, unmarried, and keeping house for her
father.

4th. ALONZO H., born June 27, 1841, in Otsego,
married Sarah Camp January 24, 1869, settled in
Evans, and has two children: 1st, CORA E., born July
20, 1872; 2d, FRANK H., born September 22, 1876. His
wife died September 27, 1891.

5th. EDGAR P., born August 15, 1845, in Otsego,
married Betsy Camp October 13, 1867, settled in ——
Erie Co., and had four children: 1st, MAUD A., born
May 7, 1869, and died May 26, 1887, aged 18; 2d,
CHARLES E., born November 2, 1873, and living unmar-

ried; 3d, WILBER A., born September 20, 1875, and living unmarried; 4th, FRED M., born November 21, 1882, and living.

6th. ELLA O.,-born July 4, 1854, and died unmarried, March 15, 1871, aged 17.

The widow and mother, Roxanna Tanner, is still very well and active, 80 years old, and keeping house for her son Alonzo

Section Twelfth. IRA—twelfth child of Ira Tanner—was born in 1811, on "the Hill," was trained a farmer but later for several years followed the seas. August 26, 1849, he married Mary Ann Soule of Maryland, N. Y., and settled on the old farm. He had four children and after a quiet and industrious life, passed away, August 2, 1856, aged 45. His widow is still living in 1892.

His children were:

1st. NANCY, born May 30, 1850, in Otsego, married Dan L. Hinds, October 12, 1870, settled in Clayville, had six children and is still living.

Her children are: 1st, CLARENCE D., born in 1872; 2d, FRANK E., born in 1873, died April 4, 1892, of pneumonia, aged 19; 3d, IRA H., born in 1875; 4th, ELLA L., born in 1878; 5th, FANNY N., born in 1889; 6th, GRACE, born in April, 1891.

2d. EMORY, born in October, 1851, married Amelia Chapin, October 23, 1872, settled near Fly Creek, has two children and is still living.

His children are: 1st, LENA, adopted, and 2d, ELLA, born in 1878 but their history is not known.

3d. ELLEN L., born in December, 1853, married February 23, 1878, John C. Williams, settled in Otsego and has no children.

4th. IRA H., born in 1856 and died February 25, 1874, unmarried, in his 18th year.

Section Thirteenth. WILLIAM—thirteenth child of Ira Tanner—was born June 18, 1813, on "the Hill," and never married. Spent his early and middle life on his father's farm, spent one year, about 1860, in Russell, then some years on the old homestead and his last days in Clayville with Nancy Hinds, his niece, where he died April 14, 1892, aged 79.

He was a quiet, worthy and christian man. During his last ten years he read the Bible through sixty-eight times.

CHAPTER IV.

THOMAS TANNER, 3D.

Thomas—second son of Thomas Tanner, Jr.,—was born in Cornwall, Conn., April 7, 1769, where he spent his boyhood amid pioneer and revolutionary scenes. In 1781 he moved with his parents to N. Lebanon, where in 1786, when only 17 years old, he married Anna Warren,* and settled for a few years. Here, soon after, both made a profession of religion and united with the church.

In 1791 he moved with his wife and child to Cooperstown, where he followed carpentry and for four years held the office of sheriff. Here he raised a large family of eight children, who were baptized by Rev. Isaac Lewis of the Presbyterian church, and received a christian training. After a residence here of eighteen years, in 1809 he moved with his family to DeKalb and settled on a farm near Tanner Creek,† and followed both farming and his trade. Here his family grew up to man and womanhood, obtained their later education, married

---

*Anna Warren's ancestry is not known, but she was doubtless a native of Massachusetts, where the Warrens were prominent, some of whose members early became distinguished, and later became numerous.

† His small, unpainted frame house was still standing in 1875, but is now torn down. This creek was formerly a large, rapid stream, passing through much wild, rocky and picturesque scenery, and affording power for a saw mill.

and many of them settled about him, and here, under the labors of Rev. James Johnson, himself and wife, with four or five other families united in forming, about 1817, the Presbyterian church of East DeKalb.

And now, in 1827, after another eighteen years residence in this adopted town, he removed with his wife and son Warren to Attica Center, Wyoming county, where his sons William and Joseph had preceded him, and settled again until 1836, when he buried his wife. The balance of his days he spent with his son William, in christian patience and waiting, when, after a short illness he died July 10, 1862, at the age of 93.

He had always been well, retaining his faculties of body and mind to the last. He was a man of medium stature and strong constitution, of plain habits and marked individuality. His life was honest and upright, his mind and conversation pure and pleasant. He was a consistent and devoted christian, a member of the Presbyterian church of Attica, and was loved and venerated by the whole community.

Section First. HARRY—oldest child of Thomas Tanner—was born April 17, 1788, in N. Lebanon and when a child moved with his parents, in 1791, to Cooperstown, where he obtained a limited education. Again in 1809, when 21 years old, he moved to DeKalb, served in the war of 1812 at Ogdensburg, and on his return married Olive Edson of the same town in 1815, and settled in Hermon; followed farming and raised a family of seven children. His wife dying in 1842, he married a Mrs. Palmer of Canton, in 1844, by whom he had one son, and she dying in 1850–1, he married again Mrs. Lent of Herman in 1854, who died west in 1888. He held several town offices, as post-master and supervisor, drew a pension many years and died April 15, 1880, aged 92, and was buried in Hermon. He was a large, heavy man, a good citizen and much respected by his neighbors.

His children were as follows:

1st. WILLIAM E., born in 1816 in Hermon, married Fanny Sutherland September 1, 1836, settled in the same town and followed shoemaking, and had three children. Many years later he settled in Canton, buried his first wife in August, 1876, and married again, Mrs. Jane D. Sims, March 11, 1879, who still survives. After spending a useful and christian life, he died June 29, 1883, aged 67.

His children were: 1st, HENRY F., born October 17, 1842, married Clara Follet, settled in Wisconsin, and is still living; 2d, MELISSA A., born August 23, 1846, and died July 19, 1876; 3d, HARWOOD D., born April 14, 1850; married Eugenie Smith June 10, 1866, settled in Wisconsin and is still living.

2d. CAROLINE, born in 1820, married Wm. B. Rose, a miller, February 16, 1843; settled in Russell many years, but in 1883 moved to Middlebury, Vt., where she is still living. He had three children: 1st, IRWIN H., born May 6, 1844, married, had one child, and died in March, 1876; 2d, LAURA M., born September 17, 1846, and died in infancy; 3d, a daughter born May 7, 1848, and died in infancy.

3d. FRANCIS, born in 1822, went to Buffalo, married Harriet Powell, "a lovely lady," settled there, followed railroading, had three or four children, and died about 1864, aged 42. His children's names and history are not known.

4th. MELISSA, born in September, 1824, in Hermon, where she died, unmarried, in the autumn of 1843, aged 19.

5th. BURNHAM, born in November, 1827, in Hermon, and died, unmarried, in June, 1847, aged 19.

6th. HARRY, born in November, 1829, never married, traveled many years with the Barker family as concert singer, and resides now near Lynn, Mass.

7th. OLIVE A., born in December, 1836, in Hermon, married Joel Olmstead in June, 1859, settled in Potsdam on a farm, had two children, and buried her husband in February, 1892.

Her children are: 1st, RHODA C., born in 1860, married Arthur C. Ames, and settled in native town; 2d, LAURA M., born about 1862-4, and died, unmarried, in June, 1883, aged about 20.

8th. PALMER, born in December, 1845, and died, unmarried, in June, 1867, aged 22.

Section Second.—WILLIAM—second son of Thomas Tanner—was born in 1791, in Cooperstown, where he obtained his early education under Oliver Cory, and learned the tanner's trade of James Averill, and married Olive Andrews * January 12, 1812. In the spring

---

* Olive was probably daughter of Wm. Andrews of Cooperstown, editor of " Impartial Observer."

of the same year he moved to Attica Center, Wyoming county, settled on a farm and also followed the tanning business. Having raised a family of seven children and his wife dying October 9, 1830, he married again, Vallonia R. Garretsel in 1831, by whom he had four children. Having spent a useful and industrious life he died September 11, 1863, aged 72. He was a respected citizen, a good christian man and member of the Presbyterian church at Attica.

His children were:

1st. ANNA E., born December 7, 1813, in Attica, married Ethan Bartlett of Orangeville, a physician, in 1831, where she settled and had five children, and died December 15, 1846, aged 33.

Her children were: 1st, NANCY E., born in 1832, died in January, 1869; 2d, MARY T., born in 1834, married a Mr. Smith; 3d, SARAH A., born in 1836, and is a teacher in Warsaw; 4th, THOMAS R., born in 1841, and died in April, 1867, aged 26; 5th, GEORGE A., born in 1843, and is a teacher in Albany.

2d. NANCY, born March 24, 1816, and died young, September 1, 1830, aged 14.

3d. THOMAS W., born October 8, 1818, in Attica, married Mary A. Webster January 15, 1840, and had four children, and is still living in Attica Center on the old homestead.

His children were: 1st, EMMA E., born May 8, 1842, married R. S. Hatch of Warsaw November 7, 1867, settled on a farm in Wilson, and has four children: DORA E., born August 21, 1868; ETTA B., born May 14, 1871;

MARY E., born November 3, 1872; CHANNIE R., born
June 1, 1879; 2d, GEORGE WILLIAM, born December 3,
1844, in Attica, married Adaline Benham in November,
1865, has three children: ELLA A., born in February,
1867, married Seth Lindsley of Attica; ELISHA W.,
born in May, 1869, married Ida Weber of Attica in
1890; MARY E., born May 1, 1875, and is unmarried;
3d, ELLA A., born November 26, 1855, and died young
January 30, 1863, aged 7; 4th, MARY A., born October
7, 1860, and died young May 6, 1882, aged 22,
unmarried.

4th. JOSEPH R., born March 10, 1821, in Attica,
married Lydia Nichols about 1845–50, settled in
Buffalo, was many years a druggist, had two children,
and died in June, 1891, aged 70. He was a member
and deacon of the Presbyterian church of the city.

His children were: 1st. WILLIAM, born about
1851–2, married Mary J. Knight of Attica, settled in
White Water, Mich., was a physician and had two
daughters; 2d. FLORENCE, born about 1855, followed
teaching and then married a carpenter, a good man,
since died, but she is still living.

5th. MARY J., born December 18, 1823, married
Wilson Knight of Attica, where she settled, had three
children and died. Her children were, MAGGIE, HEN-
RIETTA and IDA, of whom nothing more is known.

6th. OLIVE, born March 5, 1826, and died unmarried December 31, 1861, aged 35.

7th. ANDREW J., born September 9, 1826, married
Mary J. Sherman of Alexandria, Ohio, in May, 1859,

settled in Berlin, Wis., works in an office, had three children and is still living.

His children were: 1st, WILLIAM A., born March 4, 1862, married Kate Evans of Chicago, settled in Marinette, Wis.; has no children; and is a merchant; 2d, FRED E., born November 3, 1866, died February 28, 1885; 3d, MARY E:, born December 5, 1870, and is a teacher in Duluth, Minn.

William's children by second wife:

1st. EDWARD P., born September 20, 1832, never married, settled in New York as a grocer, and died December 18, 1881, aged 49.

2d. JAMES H., born October 15, 1834, married Jerusha Freeman of Bethany, January 1, 1858, settled in Batavia, engaged in coal business, adopted one child, and died February 25, 1892, aged 57.

3d. HARRIET D., born January 25, 1837, married Henry A. Kindall in 1856, settled for a while in Cortland, had no children, and died October 31, 1870, aged 33. She was quite literary and wrote for the magazines.

4th. HELEN M., born November 17, 1839, married Wm. C. Smith in 1867, settled in Attica, and is now in University Park, Oregon, has two children, Frank and Frederic. Mr. Smith is working in the Oregon mines, and Helen is teaching in the public schools.

Section Third. NANCY—third child of Thomas Tanner—was born in 1794 in Cooperstown, where she received her early education. In 1809 she moved with her parents to DeKalb, where she married Isaac Burnham* in 1813, and settled in Hermon. About 1835 she moved to Cleveland, Ohio, but soon returned. She raised a family of eleven children, and died in August, 1871, aged 77. Nancy was a Christian woman, a member of the DeKalb Presbyterian church, a faithful wife and a good mother.

Her children were as follows:.

1st. ELISHA, born March 23, 1814, in Hermon, married Mary Phelps of Richville in December, 1840, settled in Hermon, kept hotel, had five children, and died November 17, 1890, aged 76.

His children were: 1st, ADELIA, born October 5. 1841, married James Kelley, settled in Hermon, and had five children: ALLIE, EVA, FRANK, and two others; 2d, JAMES E., born April 30, 1843, and died in 1884: 3d, ISAAC M., born December 2, 1844, and died in 1865: 4th, FRANKLIN E., born October 14, 1846, and died in 1871; 5th, EDGAR S., born September 22, 1853, and married Helen Derby December 25, 1876, and settled in Hermon.

2d. MARY, born in February 1816, married Joseph Potter, settled in Joliet, Ill., had two sons, and died there June 12, 1868.

The names and history of the two sons are not known.

---

*Isaac was son of Major Burnham, native of Massachusetts, and English, who about 1809, settled in Ogdensburg and later moved to Cleveland, and died there. Isaac, born about 1790, was one of four children, viz.: Artemissia, who married John Cleghorn ; Clara, who married Woodhouse, and Olive, who married Humphrey Cleghorn. Isaac served in the "war of 1812," and died in 1851.

3d. NANCY M., born February 16, 1818, and died unmarried October 28, 1851, aged 33.

4th. LOUISA, born December 2, 1820, married Deacon Hubbard, settled in Ohio, near Cleveland, had two children, and died there.

Her children were: CLARRIE, who married in Joliet, and WILLIE, history unknown.

5th. ARTAMISIA, born October 18, 1823, married Marcus A. Brown between 1842–4, settled at Parma Center, Ohio, and has a large family, but their names are not known.

6th. CLARISSA, born October 14, 1826, and died in infancy.

7th. HARRY, her twin, born October 14, 1826, married twice and settled in Ohio and has a family of children there.

8th. ISAAC, born February 19, 1829, married Lucina Meacham, settled in Ohio and has children there, but their names are not known.

9th. EMILY A., born August 19, 1831, married George Pooler between 1850–55, settled in DeKalb, had two children, and died November 13, 1880, aged 49.

Her children were: 1st, CLARENCE, and 2d, INESS A., who married a Newell.

10th. HARRIET, born March 22, 1834, and married Edwin Alexander about 1855–60, and settled in Hermon, had two children and died June 10, 1886, aged 52.

Her children are, 1st, HARRY I., who lives in Richmond, Va., 2d, another, name not known.

11th. WILLIAM, born June 1, 1838, never married,

.served in the civil war, was taken prisoner and died in Andersonville, June 21, 1864, aged 26.

Section Fourth. LOUISA—fourth child of Thomas Tanner—was born about 1798 in Cooperstown, moved with her parents to DeKalb, and married King Follett, a Mormon deacon, between 1820–25, had two children, and about 1835 moved to Kirtland, Ohio, and joined the Mormon church* sharing its fortunes; in 1848 she went to Utah. At a later period, leaving her husband, she returned to Milton, Iowa, where she was residing in 1889, and where her son and daughter are supposed to be living.

Section Fifth. JERUSHA—fifth child of Thomas Tanner—was born in December, 1800, in Cooperstown, and in early life moved with her parents to DeKalb. Here she married Pelatiah Stacy,* January 28, 1819, and settled near "old DeKalb" on a farm. She raised a large family of twelve children, and having finished her work, died June 30, 1877, aged 76, her husband preceding her four years.

She was a woman of great energy and industry, an

---

* The Mormons began making disciples in western New York about 1830, but soon moved to Kirtland, O., where they settled in large numbers and built a temple. Driven thence a few years later, they moved o Missouri and then to Illinois, where they built the city of Nauvoo. In 1848 they emigrated to Utah, organized an independent church and state, which has since been subjected to the United States government.

* Pelatiah was a son of Isaac and Martha A. Stacy, a native of New England, who moved to Cooperstown between 1790–92, an early settler and patron of learning. In 1804 he removed to DeKalb and died there. Pelatiah, born in 1792, was the sixth of eleven children, a man of great resolution, patriotic and public-spirited, a prosperous farmer and professing christian, who died much lamented, February 24, 1872, aged 80.

earnest and active christian, a member of the Presbyterian church from girlhood, and a faithful wife and mother.

Her children were as follows:

1st. JAMES, born February 27, 1822, married Caroline Smith June 1846, settled in DeKalb, as a farmer, had four children, and died November 2, 1858, in Anamosa, Iowa, aged 36.

His children are: 1st, ARTIE, born November 17, 1847; 2d, JANE, born November 20, 1849; 3d, FLORENCE, born October 24, 1851; 4th, FREEMAN, born February 5, 1854. Of their marriage, settlement and families nothing has been learned.

2d. JERUSHA, born March 24, 1824, married D. Hills December 24, 1849, settled in DeKalb, had one child, and still living in Edwards.

Her child, MAY, born July 10, 1853, married William Little in 1877.

3d. LYDIA, born March 20, 1826, married William Matteson January 1, 1852, settled in DeKalb, had two children and is still living.

Her children are: MINNIE, born October 1, 1856, and ATTA E., born in April, 1860.

4th. WILLIAM M., born August 13, 1828, married Emily Percy February 5, 1856, settled in DeKalb as a farmer, had seven children, and died in January, 1892, aged 64.

His children are: 1st, CLARA, born July 4, 1857, married L. Cahoon, in 1876; 2d, GEORGE A., born April 27, 1859, married Minnie Johnson; 3d, ADA II., born

April 22, 1861, married B. Madison in 1884; 4th, CORA E., born July 21, 1863, married H. Miller; 5th, HETTIE M., born January 19, 1866, married J. Percy in 1891; 6th, LESLIE W., born July 15, 1868; 7th, C. R., born November 30, 1873.

5th. ISAAC W., born August 25, 1830, married Sarah A. Johnson February 5, 1856, settled in Gouverneur, as a farmer, had five children, and is still living.

His children are: 1st, CARRIE M., born November 14, 1857, and died in July, 1868; 2d, MAY G., born November 5, 1859, married A. A. Murray September 14, 1886, and has children; 3d, ELMER A., born October 21, 1862; 4th, WILLIAM P., born March 20, 1864; 5th, ATTA E., born October 24, 1875.

6th. JOHN S., born May 13, 1833, married Charlotte A. Kellogg November 16, 1862, settled in Anamosa, Iowa, is an attorney, and has four children.

His children are: 1st, EDSON E., born about 1863, and is married; 2d, MARION L., born about 1865, and married W. D. Skinner, physician; 3d, BERTHA S., born about 1867-8; 4th, WILLIAM K., born about 1870.

7th. ERASTUS W., born April 4, 1835, married Sarah A. Drury September 7, 1862, settled in DeKalb, is a farmer, and had four children.

They are: 1st, PEARL, born January 12, 1868, died March 1, 1886; 2d, BERTHA, born May 4, 1870; 3d, BESSIE, born in January, 1873; 4th, FRANKIE, born July 10, 1880.

8th. MARY A., born October 1, 1837, married

Owen Murray September 7, 1864, settled in Hermon, has two children, and is living.

They are: 1st, GEORGE W., born September 27, 1865, married Jennie Eggleston in 1891; 2d, FRANK E., born March 19, 1870, and is unmarried.

9th. ELISHA H., born May 4, 1840, married Anna S. Benton of Canton, February 22, 1864, settled near Anamosa, Ia., had five children, and still living.

His children are: 1st, HATTIE B., born June 9, 1869, married Milton E. Beck, March 6, 1890, and settled near her parents; 2d, FRANK T., born March 20, 1871, and died January 29, 1872; 3d, JOHN S., born December 27, 1872, and living; 4th, CLINTON W. born March 31, 1876, and died May 4, 1878; 5th, HELEN L., born November 9, 1880, and living.

10th. MARIA C., born February 14, 1843, married Charles E. Green, minister, April 18, 1878, settled in DeKalb, had two children, and died in October, 1889, aged 46. She had spinal curvature. Her children are: 1st, John A., born July 9, 1879; 2d, CARL S., born April 3, 1881.

11th. EDSON E., born July 29, 1845, enlisted in the civil war, and died in the service October 2, 1864, aged 19.

12th. CHARLES P., born October 4, 1848, married Francis H. Abell, at Anamosa, Ia., November 20, 1870, settled in Chicago in 1888, is traveling salesman and has two children: 1st, HOBERT A., born October 6, 1873, and unmarried; 2d, GEORGE B., born April 8, 1878, and unmarried.

5

Section Sixth. JOSEPH—sixth child of THOMAS
TANNER—was born March 23, 1803, in Cooperstown,
and in 1812 moved with his brother William to Attica.
He married Florilla Tooley February 28, 1828, settled in
the same town and followed farming twenty years; had
here three children, then in 1848 moved to Springville,
Erie county, engaged in mercantile business and died
October 11, 1873, aged 70, his wife dying three years
before. Both were members of the Presbyterian
church.

His children were as follows:

1st. ANNA L., born October 25, 1829, married
George E. Bensley, February 20, 1850, and settled in
Chicago in 1862, and had four children.

Her children are: 1st, CHARLES R., born October
7, 1852, married Emma Excell of Brooklyn October 7,
1873, where he is supposed to have settled; had five
children, moved onto a peach farm near South Haven,
Mich., in 1888, and died December 25, 1889.
His children are: CLARIE E., GEORGE E. JR., ROY
E., NORMATHALL, and one dying in infancy. They
are living with their mother on the peach farm; 2d,
ELLA F., born September 30, 1856, Married George H.
Pierce of Chicago, February 12, 1884, settled in Chicago, and is now living with her parents, and has one
child, MARION L., born May 11, 1888; 3d, LOTTIE C.,
born between 1858–60, and died when she was three
years old; 4th, GEORGE E., born in October, 1860–62,
and died in infancy.

2d. RICHARD W., born June 5, 1832, married

Marinda Haskins December 31, 1856, settled in Springville in mercantile business, had five children, and is still living.

His children were: 1st, ANNA F., born February 28, 1859, and died August 15, 1890, aged 31; 2d, ALLEN J., born June 17, 1863, married Mary Henry June 10, 1891; 3d, HARRY W., born May 24, 1868, married Nellie B. Lowe December 14, 1891; 4th, CLARK W., born January 20, 1872; 5th, GRACE H., born May 6, 1874.

3d. CHARLES J., born April 4, 1837, married Louisa Bundy January 15, 1862; now settled in Chicago, engaged in the live-stock business, and has one child; GEORGIA E., born May 10, 1864, married John R. Woodbridge July 16, 1887, and has one child, HELEN L., born November 15, 1889.

Section Seventh. LUCAS—seventh child of Thomas Tanner—was born in Cooperstown, January 10, 1805, moved thence to DeKalb, where he received an elementary education, and married Sophrona Ames of Canton, about 1835, settled in Hermon and followed farming and had four children. In 1852, affected by the prevalent "gold fever of California," he started thither, "via the cape," but died at sea August 11, aged 47. He was an active and excellent christian man and his untimely death much lamented.

His children were as follows:

1st. BETSEY, born about 1836 in Hermon, married a Mr. Miles between 1856–8, had no children, and died some years since.

2d. MARIA, born in 1839, in Hermon, married Richard Allen in 1860, settled in Canton, had two children, and is still living.

Her children are: 1st, M. H. ALLEN, born in 1861 in Canton, and settled in Chicago in business; 2d, IDA M. ALLEN, born in 1866 in Canton, where she is still living—not married.

3d. LOUISA, born in 1842 in Hermon, married George Ingalls about 1863, settled in Canton, had one child, and is still living.

Her child is: FRANK, born in 1864 in Canton, where he is living.

4th. FRANK, born in 1844 in Hermon, married Josie M. Lawrence in April, 1867, settled now in Cedar Rapids, Iowa, is in mercantile business, and had three children.

His children are: 1st, CHARLES L., born in 1868 in Cedar Rapids, where he is still living; 2d, FRANKIE, born in 1869, and died in infancy; 3d, BESSIE, born in 1871 in Cedar Rapids, and now living there.

Section Eighth. WARREN — eighth child of Thomas Tanner—was born in 1809, probably in De-Kalb, where he received his early training and education, and grew up to manhood beside the woods, rocks and glens of Tanner Creek. In 1827 he moved with his parents to Attica, and here, though suffering from feeble health, he followed teaching. He died unmarried in February, 1836, aged 27. He was an excellent christian man " the very salt of the earth."

CHAPTER V.

ZERA TANNER.

ZERA — third son of Thomas Tanner — was born in 1770 in Cornwall, Conn., and hence a mere child during the Revolution. After the war he moved with his parents to New Lebanon, Conn., and thence about 1790 went to Granville. Here he met Jenette McWhorter,* whom he married in 1792–3. Near 1795 he moved with his family to Cooperstown, where he resided fourteen years, followed farming, and where five of his eight children were born. In 1809 he removed to Warsaw,† Wyoming county, and settled on a new farm on West Hill, two miles from the village and near his father-in-law. Here he resided and toiled until his death in November, 1837, dying suddenly of heart disease while sitting at supper, aged 67, his wife dying the next January at the same age. Soon after their arrival they both united with the Presbyterian church on profession, near the date of its organization, and lived quiet and consistent Christians and good citizens till their decease. His children were as follows:

Section First. POLLY—first child of Zera Tanner

---

* Jenette was daughter of John McWhorter, of Scotch-Irish ancestry, who early married and settled in Hebron, and later in Granville, and thence in 1807 moved to Warsaw. She was born in 1771, the third of seven children and sister of Samuel, the first school teacher and justice in Warsaw, and occupant of several county and state offices.

† See Appendix F.

—was born January 7, 1795, in Granville, whence she moved with her parents to Cooperstown and thence in 1809 to Warsaw. Here she obtained a common school education, and married Lewis Wood * January 17, 1813, settled near Olean till 1823-4, then in Portageville till 1836, and last in Sharon Center. She had ten children, and after an arduous and useful life, died July 7, 1859, aged 64, and her husband in 1865. Their religious profession was that of Universalist.

Her children were as follows:

1st. SUSAN E., born April 13, 1815, in Olean, and died unmarried, January 27, 1877, aged 62.

2d. LOUISA, born July 10, 1817, in Olean, married James R. Barnes about 1840, in Portageville, where she settled, then at Millgrove, Cincinnati, and Nunda, where she died May 20, 1864, aged 47.

She had four children: 1st, MARY, who married Frank Wager of Buffalo, and has four children; 2d, LEWIS, who married in Nunda, and has three children; 3d, ARTHUR, who married in St. Louis, and has two children; 4th, ALBERT, who died unmarried.

3d. MARY JANET, born February 22, 1820, in Olean, married first Abel Rose, September 22, 1840, and settled in Millgrove and Sharon Centre, and had two children; married second Clark Carrier, in 1851, in

---

* Lewis was son of Wheelock Wood and Lydia Murdock, who were married in 1784, in Uxbridge, Mass., their native town, where he was born October 15, 1787. In early life he moved to western New York, where he found his companion. After filling various spheres of useful and public life as lumberman and legislator, he passed away September 25, 1865 aged 78.

the latter town, and had one child; married third Daniel Dodge, February 22, 1858, in the same town, and is still living.

Her children are: 1st, HARRY A. ROSE, born December 15, 1842, married Ada Peabody of Ceres, and has four children; 2d, EDWIN V. ROSE, born in May, 1844, married Emma Glinis, and has no children; 3d, LEWIS C. CARRIER, born 1852, married Cerie Brock of Ceres, and had two daughters and one son.

4th. NANCY E., born May 27, 1822, in Olean, married September 22, 1843, John Tingley, a farmer and inventor, settled in Portageville, Sharon Centre, and Philadelphia, had four children and is still living.

Her children are: 1st, FLORENCE E., born April 27, 1845, married John E. Dillenger in 1865, and has one child, STELLA; 2d, MONROE W., born December 12, 1850, married Maria C. Quibil of Philadelphia, January 1, 1880, and has one child, JULIAN; 3d, PHILO B., born December 9, 1857, married first Josie Creede, in 1887; second Alice Parent, in 1889, and has no children; 4th, HELEN M., born August 16, 1854, married Herman S. Rice, January 1, 1880, of Portville, and has no children.

5th. EVILINE E., born May 17, 1824, in Portageville, married between 1844-6 Jacob B. Saxe, Universalist minister, settled last in Fort Scott, Kansas, had four children, and died in 1881, aged 57.

Her children were: 1st, MARY, married and settled in Fort Scott; 2d, EVA; 3d, EDWIN; 4th, NETTIE.

6th. JULIA, born October 1, 1826, and died in infancy.

7th. PERMELIA, born March 4, 1829, in Portageville, married William H. Chaddock about 1840, jeweler, colonel in United States Army, and car manufacturer, settled in Warsaw, and last in Annisbon, Ala., had two children, and died South August 28, 1888, aged 59.

Her children were: 1st, NELLIE, unmarried; 2d, ISABEL, married Frank Murch of Jersey City, and has one child.

8th. JANE, born August 2, 1831, and died in infancy.

9th. LEWIS N., born March 4, 1833, in Portageville, married between 1853–5 Eliza Este of Sharon Centre, where they settled and had three children. He served in the civil war, and was killed May 10, 1864, aged 31.

His children were: 1st, FOREST E., married Alice Jackson, and lives in DeGolia, Pa.; 2d, LEWIS J., married Jennie Lyman, and lives in Roulette, Pa.; 3d, LIZZIE, married A. E. Stickler, and lives in Farmer's Valley, Pa.

10th. EDWIN V., born April 17, 1836, in Portageville, married Olive B. Glinis July 9, 1863, in Sharon Centre, where they settled, and later in Ceres, has had four children, and is living.

His children are: 1st, EVA G., born June 30, 1864, and died in infancy; 2d, WILLIAM, born March 4, 1866, and living unmarried; 3d, CHARLES, born October 16, 1868, unmarried; 4th, NINA, born October 8, 1881.

Section Second. CYRUS—second child of Zera Tanner—was born December 11, 1797, in Cooperstown,. moved with his parents in 1809, through the wilderness, to Warsaw, where he was educated, and grew up on a. new farm, married Jane A. Spencer * May 11, 1826, and later settled on his father's farm in Warsaw, and raised five children. In May, 1868, he suddenly died of heart disease, as did his father, at the age of 71. Himself and wife were members of the Presbyterian church of Warsaw.

His children were as follows:

1st. ISABEL E, born February 17, 1827, married Elizar W. Norton, in December, 1846, and settled near Warsaw, had two children, and died January 27, 1850, aged 23.

Her children were: 1st, ELLA, born in 1848, married Daniel Keeney between 1868 and '70, settled in Warsaw, and had four children, ARTHUR, CORA, EDNA, and WALTER; 2d, ISABEL, born January 20, 1850, married E. Jewell between 1870–5, had two sons, and died a few years ago.

2d. CORDELIA, born January 2, 1831, in Warsaw, married Hiram Rich August 7, 1862, settled in Belfast, N. Y., and has two children.

Her children were: 1st, CHARLES, born September 28, 1864, married Minnie Marsh October 7, 1885, settled in Belfast, clerk in store, and has two children, LEOLA, born November 4, 1886, and CHARLES, born in 1888;

---

* Jane Ann was daughter of Phineas and Elsie Spencer. resident of Greenville, New York, where she was born June 26, 1803, and where she was raised and married, Her death was in January, 1886.

2d, WILLIAM M., born March 13, 1866, married Hattie Gleason, March 4, 1885, settled in Moravia, a mechanic, has two children, ANNA M., born in 1885, and Robert G., born in 1890.

3d. LAURA, born in 1832, and died in infancy.

4th. EDWARD, born April 18, 1834, in Warsaw, married Charity Maranville November 9, 1856, settled in his native town, has two children, and is still living.

His children were: 1st, ISABEL, born June 30, 1857, married George Taylor, settled in Warsaw, and has one child, CORA; 2d, MARIAN, born February 1, 1862, married Will Purdy, but was left a widow, and is living with her father.

5th. MARY A., born February 20, 1838, in Warsaw, married Artemus T. Benson May 18, 1862, settled at Cattaraugus Station, has three children, and is still living.

Her children are: 1st, ELIZABETH, who married Frank Weidner, settled in Buffalo, and has one child, GRACE A.; 2d, FANNIE; 3d, NELLIE, both living at home unmarried.

Section Third. REBECCA — third child of Zera Tanner — was born in Cooperstown October 31, 1800, when a child moved with her parents to Warsaw, and grew up under pioneer surroundings. She married Warren Webster * December 29, 1819, and settled on a

---

* Warren was son of Elihu Webster, a native of Connecticut, who early settled in Hampton, and then in 1803 moved to Warsaw and took up land. Warren was born in November, 1795, was educated in Warsaw, was justice of the peace in Orangeville, elder of the Presbyterian church in Ripley and Gowanda, and died in the latter town January 27, 1864, aged 69.

farm in Orangeville, where several of her children were born. In 1833-4 she moved to Franklin, Pa., thence to Ripley, N. Y., and later to Gowanda, where her husband died. She had ten children, five of whom died young, spent her last years in Westfield with her daughter Martha, and died April 20, 1879, aged 78. She was an intelligent, interesting and christian woman, and member of the Presbyterian church, When 70 years old, she wrote a beautiful poem for her family.

Her children were:

1st. WALTER, born in 1821 in Orangeville, married Mary Johnson in 1845-6, and settled in Gowanda, engaged in leather and shoe business, then, in 1862, moved to Bushnell, Ill., had five children, and died there of consumption.

His children were: 1st, CHARLES, who died in infancy; 2d, MARY L., born July 5, 1848, in Gowanda, married George W. Burpee of Bushnell in 1866, where she is still living; 3d, HELEN R., who died at 5 years; 4th, CARLTON W., who died at 2 years; 5th, WALTER, JR., born December 31, 1864, in Bushnell, where he is living.

2d. JENNETTE, born in 1826 in Orangeville, married Dwight Dickson about 1850, settled in Ripley, had four children, and died of consumption July 30, 1860, aged 34.

Her children were: 1st, WALTER H., born April 8, 1852; 2d, WARREN W., born July 14, 1854, married Sadie Arnold in 1878, and has two children; 3d, ADA J., who died in infancy; 4th, CARLTON A., born May 4, 1860.

3d.   MARTHA A., born in 1830, and died at 5 years.

4th.   WILLIAM P., born in 1834 in Ripley, married Lucy F. Perry of Gowanda, had one son, now living, and died March 21, 1864, aged 34.

5th.   MARTHA, born in 1837 in Ripley, married A. M. Miniger of Ripley June 12, 1867, has two children, and now resides in Westfield.

Her children are: 1st, GEORGE W., born February 9, 1871, in Ripley, and is unmarried; 2d, MATTIE E., born October 17, 1875, in Westfield, and is unmarried.

6th.   ALBERT S., born about 1840, and died in infancy.

7th.   ALBERT II., born in 1844, and died at 16 of consumption.

Section Fourth.   IRA—fourth child of Zera Tanner —was born in Cooperstown November 9, 1802, when a child moved with his parents to Warsaw, and died in 1813, while still a mere youth.

Section Fifth.   ELIZA—fifth child of Zera Tanner —was born in Cooperstown July 3, 1805, moved with her parents in 1809 to Warsaw, where, under primitive surroundings, she received her early education. She married Eli Rood * of Wethersfield, May 11, 1826, where she settled, had three children, and died October 21, 1840, aged 35.

Her children were as follows:

1st.   ZERA T., born February 21, 1827, married

---

* Eli was a son of David and Sarah Rood, native of Vermont; was born October 31, 1797, came to Wethersfield in 1817, where he settled, and died in 1877, aged 80.

Rosetta Brown in 1849, settled in Wethersfield Spa., had four children, and is now living in Grand Rapids, Michigan.

His children are: 1st, ELIZA, born about 1850, married Smith Scoville and settled in Warsaw; 2d, LORA, born about 1852, married Americus Pruer and settled in Warsaw; 3d, CLARA, born about 1854, and died young; 4th, FRANK, born about 1856, and is supposed to be living in Grand Rapids.

2d. DAVID P., born July 21, 1829, married Elizabeth Boddy, February 26, 1850, and had one child. His wife dying in 1855, he married again Nancie A. Truesdell, October 7, 1856, settled in Wethersfield, was in the civil war, had three children, and buried his wife in 1885. He married third, Helen A. Royce, November 9, 1887, had one son, and is living in Johnsonburg. Mr. Rood served three years in the civil war, was promoted to second lieutenant, and wounded at the battle of Cold Harbor.

His children are: 1st, ELI, born October 20, 1851, married Kate Mahanny, about 1876, and had four children, HELEN, born in 1877, NORMAN, born in 1879, MAMIE, born in 1883, and CHARLEY, born in 1885. Eli now resides at Suspension Bridge; 2d, MARY E., born August 5, 1867, married Adelbert Cook, settled in Wethersfield Spa., has three children and is still living. Her children are: MABEL N., born in 1886, ADA, born in 1889, and WILLIE, born in 1891; 3d, DORA B., born August 8, 1869, married William Burch May 1, 1887, settled in Warsaw and has two children, JENNIE M., born in May,

1889, and BESSIE B., born in May, 1892; 4th, LILLIAN
A., born November 29, 1876, and living with her parents;
5th, DANIEL P., JR., born November 4, 1888.

3d. HELEN E., born March 13, 1832, married
Warren B. Morgan about 1850, had two children, and
died July 17, 1854.

Her children are: 1st, CHARLES, born in 1852, and
living in Clinton, Iowa; 2d, EMELINE, born in 1854,
married Wm. Hatfield and settled in Warsaw, and has
no children.

Section Sixth. CLARISSA — sixth child of Zera
Tanner — was born October 21, 1807, in Cooperstown,
and when 2 years old moved with her parents to Warsaw, where she received a common school education.
She married Lemuel Smith* of Portageville July 3,
1828, where she settled till 1834, when she moved to
Portville. She raised four children, an1 having served
her family and age, fell asleep in 1883, aged 76. She
was a bright, energetic woman; a faithful wife and good
mother.

Her children are as follows:

1st. SARAH S., born March 28, 1829, in Portageville, married Andrew L. Rice July 26, 1850, settled in
Portville, had four children, and is still living there.

Her children are: 1st, HIRAM L., born January 16,
1852, married Helen M. Tingley January 1, 1880, lives
in Portville, and has no children; 2d, BUTLER II., born

* Lemuel, son of Seth Smith of Canada, his native place, and born
between 1804-6, was one of three children, Nathan and Sophia being his
brother and sister, who moved with their parents about 1813-15 to New
York. He died in 1884 in Portville, aged about 80.

November 28, 1853, and is unmarried; 3d, UNA E., born July 6, 1860, and is deceased; 4th, HARRIET E., born June 21, 1871, and is unmarried.

2d. HIRAM B., born August 6, 1831, in Portageville, married Charlotte M. Percival of Charleston, S. C., June 13, 1857, where he settled till the beginning of the civil war, when he came North and settled in Olean.

He had six children: 1st, JULIA C., born August 3, 1858, in Charleston; 2d, GRACE P., born August 27, 1862, in Olean, and married F. A. Wood of Grand Valley, Pa., September 13, 1887; 3d, MAY M., born March 22, 1864, in Olean, and remains unmarried; 4th, JESSIE A., born December 21, 1867, in Olean, married John E. Eggleston of the same town June 10, 1891; 5th, AMIE L., born September 8, 1873, and is unmarried; 6th, FRED P., born November 25, 1874, and is unmarried.

3d. JANE E., born April 7, 1835, in Portville, married Eugene L. Ruggles in 1856, now settled in LaCrosse, Wis., had four children, and is still living there.

Her children are: 1st, CLARA E., born March 30, 1857, married Charles H. Lane in 1879, is living in Charles City, Iowa, and has three children: WARREN, CLINTON and GUY; 2d, EMMA A., born in Ripon, Wis., August 30, 1860, married O. N. Schall of Charles City in 1884, had one son, EUGENE, and died much lamented September 30, 1885; 3d, HARMONY, born March 11, 1867, in Ripon, married A. W. Schall in 1886, settled in LaCrosse, and has no children; 4th, IRVING E., born

May 2, 1878, in Charles City, and is living with his parents.

4th. EMELINE M., born August 18, 1843, in Portville, married John McGraw* of Rochester about 1865, had three children, and buried her husband.

Her children are: 1st, CHARLES S., born in 1867; 2d, FRED, born in 1870; 3d, LILLIAN, born in 1874; all unmarried.

Section Seventh. ZERA—seventh child of Zera Tanner—was born August 9, 1810, in Warsaw, grew up under the hardships, scenes, and associations of a new country, married Ruth E. Foster† about 1834-5, settled in Warsaw, followed farming, had one son, and died while yet young, November 27, 1836, aged 26.

ZERA L., born December 5, 1836, when 19 engaged in the naval service and has followed the sea ever since. During the civil war he was in government service, and active in the capture of Fort Fisher. He is now commander of the United States Steamer Albatros, on the Pacific coast, with headquarters at San Francisco.

Section Eighth. EMELINE—eighth child of Zera Tanner—was born in December, 1812, grew up amid primitive scenes, and was educated in the country schools. She married Willis Pettibone about 1830, and

---

* John was son of John McGraw, of Scotch ancestry, and a wealthy lumberman of Rochester. He died December 25, 1877.

† Ruth E. was daughter of Luther and Ruth Foster, natives of Long Island, who settled in 1823 in Warsaw. Luther was a good Christian man. Ruth E. was one of ten children, sister of Julius Foster, a graduate of Hamilton College, and a Presbyterian minister.

settled in her native town.   She had one child, and died
soon, June 20, 1832, in her 20th year, death lopping the
bough in its first fruitage.

Her child MARTHA, born between 1831–2, married
Clark D. Munger of Warsaw between 1850–5, moved to
Kilbourn City, Wis., had four children, early buried
her husband, and is still living there, a widow.

Of her four children only one is living, ELLIS D.
MUNGER.

6

CHAPTER VI.

ISAAC TANNER.

ISAAC—fourth child of Thomas Tanner—was born in Cornwall in 1772, and was a small child during the period of the revolution. About 1781 he moved with his parents to New Lebanon where he obtained his early education, and thence, in 1793, to Cooperstown, then a small new town, and the country wild and woody. Here the same year he married Priscilla Davis, settled down probably on a farm, and raised three children.

In 1809 he moved with his family to DeKalb, and settled again on wild land in a new country. His first wife dying in February, 1832, a few years later he married again, and August 26, 1853 his death occurred at the age of 81. He was of medium height and corpulent, of active temperment and jovial disposition. He was called "Captain Tanner," serving perhaps in "the war of 1812," or in the State militia.

His children were as follows:

Section First. ISAAC—first child of Isaac Tanner Sr.,—was born in 1794 in Cooperstown; where he received the rudiments of an education, and whence in 1809 he moved with his parents to DeKalb. He served in "the war of 1812," being stationed at Ogdensburg. After the war closed he was engaged for several years on public works, on "the old Albany road," and in building the "Arsenal of Russell." In 1825 he married Lucretia Livingston, and some years later settled on a small farm in DeKalb, and followed farming and teaming. He had seven children when, in 1846, his wife died. He married again Phebe Jane Percy in 1849, by whom he had four children, and died at DeKalb Junction, his last residence, in 1880, aged 86.

He was a rather large, corpulent man, of social and easy-going habits.

His children were as follows:

1st. ZERA, born about 1826, remained unmarried. followed a roving life, went west and died in Wisconsin,

2d. JOHN, born about 1828, married Mary Marium, and died without issue at DeKalb Junction.

3d. LORA, born about 1830, did housework, and before the civil war went with a family to Charleston, S. C., where she is supposed to have died unmarried.

4th. WILLIAM, born about 1832, married Martha Rice, settled in Wisconsin, has five children, and is still living.

5th. ISAAC, born in 1834, married twice—his last wife was a Miss Harris—went to Minnesota, is now settled in Dakota and has three children.

6th. PRISCILLA, born in 1836, married Timothy M. Craig of Canton in 1875, where she settled, had one child, and is now living, a widow, in DeKalb Junction.

Her child, STANLEY, was born in 1877.

7th. IRA, born in 1838, enlisted in the civil war, and was killed in battle in 1861, aged 23.

8th. SARAH, born in 1851, married first Daniel

Glasby of Edwards, and had two children. He dying, she married again II. Reed, had one child, and is living.

9th. JAMES, born in 1853, married Carrie Mulligan of DeKalb in 1878, settled at the Junction, follows railroading, and has three children, GERTRUDE, BERT, and ERNEST.

10th. MARY, born in 1855, married George Babcock of DeKalb, a baggage-man, in December, 1877, and has two children, MINNIE and LESTER, and is still living.

11th. EMMA, born in 1858, married first Arthur Brown, and he dying, married second Chauncey Baker, has three children, and is still living.

Section Second. MARY (POLLY)—second child of Isaac Tanner, Sr.—was born in 1796–8, in Cooperstown, moved with her parents in 1809 to DeKalb, married Wm. Cooper* in 1826, and settled at Cooper's Falls, had one child and died young, about 1830.

MARY, her child, was born in January, 1827, married Stephen Slosson, merchant in DeKalb, about 1847, had six children, and died October 15, 1859. Her children were STEPHEN, MARY L., CHARLES, and CLIFTON, who are dead, and GEORGE and LESTER, living in New York City, the former being the noted "Champion billiard player."

Section Third. SARAH (SALLY)—third child of

---

* William was son of James Cooper, native of Burlington, New Jersey, brother of Courtland and James, nephew of Judge Wm. Cooper, and cousin of James Fenimore, the American novelist, one of a noted and numerous family. He married a second time, had one more child, and died October 24, 1858, about 65 years old.

Isaac Tanner, Sr.—was born about 1798–1800, in Cooperstown, moved with her parents to DeKalb in 1809, married Courtland Cooper in 1826, and a few years later moved to Oswego, where she died, leaving two children, EMILY and JAMES, both of whom died young.

CHAPTER VII.

ANNA TANNER WILLIAMS.

ANNA—fifth child of Thomas Tanner—was born in 1776, at Cornwall, and when a small child moved with her parents to New Lebanon, where she received her early education, and thence, in 1793, to Cooperstown. Here she married David Hatch,* physician, in 1795, and settled in the same town. By him she had two children, when, about 1798, he left her for causes not well known.

About 1800, Anna married again John Williams of Cooperstown, where she settled a few years; then in 1809 they moved to DeKalb, settled on a new farm, and raised a large family of ten children, all born in DeKalb. They early with others united in forming the First Presbyterian church of East DeKalb.

About 1840 she buried her second husband, John Williams,† and spent the balance of her days with her sons. Having spent a pioneer life of hard work, she died September 25, 1856, aged 80.

---

* Mr. Hatch, probably a native of Connecticut, went to New Orleans, married again, became wealthy, and died there.

† John was probably son of Rensselaer Williams, native of Connecticut, who, with his brother Richard, settled in Cooperstown between 1792-7, and established themselves as merchants.

The Williams family were numerous and prominent in early New England history, and several families became pioneer settlers of different towns in Otsego county.

She was a woman of great energy and endurance, of kind Christian spirit, a faithful wife and good mother.

Her children were as follows:

Section First. POLLY HATCH—first child of Anna Hatch—was born in Cooperstown in March, 1796, moved with her mother in 1809 to DeKalb, married in May, 1813, Nehemiah Barker of Russell, a farmer, settled in DeKalb, Hermon, and Rossie, also in Essex county, had ten children, and died in Russell in 1862, aged 68; her husband dying a year later.*

Her children were as follows:

1st. JANE, born November 8, 1814, in DeKalb, married Amos Keth of Rossie in June, 1836, where she settled and had four children. Her husband dying of consumption she married again Richard Allen of Canton, July 10, 1867, who died five years later. Mrs. Allen is now living in Lansing, Michigan.

Her children were: 1st, WILLIAM H., born in 1839 and died in 1860; 2d, RUTH, born in 1841 and died in 1852; 3d, SILAS, born in 1843 and died young, all three dying of consumption; 4th, ANNETTE, born May 30, 1853, married March 30, 1878, H. T. M. Treglawn, merchant in Lansing, and has three children.

2d. CLARISSA, born in February, 1816, in DeKalb, married Orley Gibbons in 1834, settled in Russell, had four children, and died in 1853, aged 37.

---

* Mr. N. Barker was born in Vermont in 1791, moved with his two brothers, Chesley and Daniel, to Russell at its first settlement, about 1813. Served as volunteer in "the war of 1812" at Ogdensburg, followed farming, and died in 1863, aged 72.

Her children were: 1st, HUBBARD; 2d, ASHLEY; 3d, SOLON; 4th, ORLEY; all married and living.

3d. ANN ELIZA, born in January, 1818, in DeKalb, married Benjamin Bull in 1836, settled in Lewis, Essex county, had four children, and died in 1874, aged 56. .

Her children are: 1st, ELLEN; 2d, MARY; 3d, JESTINE; and 4th, CHARLES; all married and living.

4th. TIMOTHY H., born May 8, 1820, in Hermon, married Caroline Freeman December 2, 1845, settled in Lewis, and had two children. His wife dying, he married again Margaret Pritchard July 4, 1854, moved to South Grove, Illinois, in 1865, had two children, and died November 20, 1875, aged 55.

His children were HENRY, PRISCILLA, and two others deceased.

5th. CHESLEY, born in 1822, in Hermon, went to California between 1855–60, married twice, had two children, and became wealthy.

6th. MILLY, born in 1824 in Hermon, married Lorenzo Harris, farmer, about 1844, moved to Wisconsin, has two children, and is still living.

Her children are MARY and WILLIE.

7th. PRISCILLA, born in 1826, married Calvin Knox of Russell, in 1852, where she settled, and had two children and died.

Her children were: 1st, HELEN, born in 1853, married Charles Smith, and has three children; 2d, JESTINE, born in 1855, married, and dead.

8th. JESTINE, born in 1828 in Hermon, married a Mr. Presby of Lewis, moved to Wisconsin and had two children, and buried her husband. She married again Presby Lowell, and is still living.

Her children are LORENZO and HARRIS, both young men grown.

9th. WILLIAM, born in 1830, married Mary Freeman of Somerville in 1856, settled in Rossie, has four children, and is a prosperous farmer.

His children are FRED, CHARLEY, WILLIE, and BERTIE, all grown up, all married but one, and settled about home.

10th. CHARLES, born in 1832, served in the civil war three years, was taken prisoner, and died in Andersonville.

Section Second. TIMOTHY B.—second child of Anna Hatch—was born June 19, 1798, moved in 1809 with his mother to DeKalb, married Martha Fuller about 1823, settled in Hermon on a farm, and had seven children, all born in that town. His wife dying, he married again Lydia Cooley, and third Sally A. Williams. After an industrious, successful, and worthy life he died June 17. 1873, aged 75.

His children were as follows:

1st. WILLIAM, born February 11, 1824, went to Wallula, Washington, married, settled, and died, leaving no heirs, October 26, 1890, aged 66.

2d. ARDELIA A., born December 25, 1825, married William D. Gilman, a carpenter, December 25, 1844, settled in Hermon, had two children, and died September 14, 1857, aged 32, her husband dying two years later.

Her children were: 1st, DERIUS, born in 1846, and died at four years; 2d, FLORENCE, born in 1848, and died at 6 years.

3d. MARGARET, born March 27, 1828, married E. D. Morgan in 1848, and settled in DeKalb on a farm, had no children, and died in March 1856, aged 28.

4th. JOHN F., born July 22, 1830, married Thyrza Hayes in 1855, settled in Moody, Franklin county, had three children, and died December 24, 1891, aged 60.

His children were BREMEN, WILLIS, and HALSEY.

5th. LURETTA, born August 25, 1833, married E. D. Maddock in 1856, and had one child. Her husband dying in 1868, she married again Charles G. Matteson, a retired farmer, February 22, 1874, and settled in Canton.

Her child, EDWARD H., born about 1857, died young, between 1863-4.

6th. MARY, born November 18, 1834, married Winslow T. Barker February 2, 1870, lawyer and circuit judge, settled in Dubuque, Iowa, had no children, and buried her husband between 1872-4. She has since resided in Washington, D. C., and engaged in office work, in the patent office department.

7th. HARRIET, born July 22, 1839, married October 1, 1856, Isaac Gibbons, merchant, had one child, and is still living.

Her child, MINNIE, born December 27, 1857, died at 5 years old.

Section 3d. ELIZA—third child of Anna Williams—born about 1801, in Cooperstown, moved with her parents to DeKalb, married Harry Stacy of the same town about 1820, and settled in Richville. In 1834 she moved to Ohio, settled on a farm, had eleven children, and died in 1836, aged 35.

Her children were as follows:

Six of them died in Ohio, and the father returned in 1843 with the other five to DeKalb, viz.:

1st. HARRY.

2d. JOHN.

3d. LIZZY, who married Smith of East DeKalb.

4th. JULIA.

5th. MARIA, who married H. H. Chandler and settled in Ogdensburg.

HARRY, JOHN, and LIZZY have since died.

Section Fourth. RENSSELAER—fourth child of Anna Williams—was born in Cooperstown in 1803, moved with his parents to DeKalb, married Catharine Randall of the same town about 1830, settled there on a farm, followed farming and teaming, had three children and died in 1849, aged 46.

His children were as follows:

1st. JOHN, born October 21, 1833, married Malinda E. Baker June 16, 1854, served three years in the civil war, then followed blacksmithing in Hermon, had three children, and burried his wife in 1872. He married again Emma M. Hamilton of Hermon, and in 1884 moved to Mankato, Minn., and engaged in insurance business.

His children are: 1st, a son, born in 1858 and died in infancy; 2d, ERINE, born in April, 1866, and now a type-writer in St. Paul; 3d, D. VERNETTE, born in July, 1867, and now a book-keeper in Mankato.

2d. DEBORAH, born July 31, 1837, married Chauncey Knox October 9, 1859. He dying in two years, she married again, Wm. E. Boyd, April 13, 1865, settled in Russel, had two children, and died January 29, 1892, aged 54.

Her children were: 1st, LUNA, born September 1, 1866, unmarried, and teaching school; 2d, LYDIA, born in 1868, and died at two years old.

3d. MARTHA, born in June, 1846, married Wm. B. Craig, in April, 1863, a merchant, and settled down in Mankato. She has no children.

Section Fifth. WILLIAM—fifth child of Anna Williams—was born in 1805, in Cooperstown, and moved with his parents to DeKalb, where he married Amanda Burnette of the same town March 5, 1828. He settled here till 1843, when he moved to Canton, raised ten children, and after a useful life, died September 13, 1885, aged 80, his wife dying five years later.

His children were as follows:

1st. MARY A., born September 25, 1824, and died unmarried January 17, 1880, aged 51.

2d. BENEDICT B., born December 12, 1831. Married Clara Cooley November 7, 1860, and settled in Dexter, Mich., and had two children, ALBERT and ANNA, and is still living.

3d. CLARA M., born July 29, 1833, married Benjamin Rose, April 14, 1859, and settled in Clarksville, Nebraska.

She has three children: 1st, FRANK; 2d, MYRA, and 3d, CORA; and is still living.

4th. AMARYLLIS, born in March, 1835, married Gardner Butterworth March 29, 1855, and settled in Canton.

She had two children: 1st, CLARA, born in 1858, and died in 1876; 2d, MARY, born in 1866, married and settled in Canton.

5th. EDGAR, born September 16, 1837, married Jane Robinson January 8, 1860, settled in Canton, and had three children. His wife dying he married again Elizabeth Sayer, February 18, 187–, and has another child.

His children are: 1st, ROSALIE, born in 1860, and died young; 2d, EDNA, born in 1870; 3d, FRANK, born in 1872; and 4th, BELLE, born in 1891.

6th. FLORINDA, born December 21, 1839, married William Anderson August 30, 1876, and settled in Selma, California.

She has two children: 1st, BESSIE, born in 1878; and 2d, FRANK, born in 1879.

7th. WILLIAM H., born December 12, 1841, served in the civil war, and was killed in the battle of the Wilderness, May 17, 1864, aged 22.

8th. JOHN B., born May 6, 1843, served in the civil war, and was killed in Petersburg August 5, 1864, aged 21.

9th. EUGENIE E., born May 16, 1845, married William Hallock January 2, 1867, and settled in Brighton, Michigan.

She has one child, WINIFRED.

10th. LESLIE A., born April 27, 1849, married Edna Adsit June 16, 1874, had one son, and his wife dying, he married again Ella Wilson in March, 1885, settled in Watertown, and has another son.

His children are: VERNON, born in 1881; and CLARENCE, born in 1886.

Section Sixth. NOAH C.—sixth child of Anna Williams—was born in February, 1807, in Cooperstown, married Sally A. Baker of Hermon, about 1832, settled in the same town as farmer, had seven children, and died September 28, 1854, aged 47. His wife survived him 35 years, and died 80 years of age.

His children were as follows:

1st. SARAH, born June 3, 1833, married Otis Earle November 12, 1851, settled in Edwards and then in Hermon, had three children, became a widow in 1877, and now lives in Gouverneur with her daughter.

Her children were: 1st, BOWER H., born January 20, 1853, in Edwards, and died in infancy, July 18, 1854; 2d, FLORENCE, born April 21, 1856, in Edwards, married Silas W. Payne of Antwerp, May 13, 1874, settled in the same town till 1883, when she moved to Gouverneur, and had three children, WEBSTER E., born March 19, 1878, and died January 12, 1882, PLINY F., born October 8, 1879, and died January 5, 1882, and FLORENCE B., born March 1, 1883; 3d, CHARLES P., born June 24, 1858, in Edwards, married Addie B. Chapin of Hermon, August 26, 1879, and settled in Gouverneur, and had three children, OTIS H., born July 27, 1881, and died December 20,

1881. in infancy, FLORENCE I., born August 5, 1886, and FRANCES I., born September 1, 1889.

2d. SAMUEL B., born in August, 1834, married Mary Matteson October 25, 1860, she dying in January, 1862, he married Nettie Baker in February, 1864, and she dying in February, 1865, he married again Mrs. Elinor Deming in March, 1867, and settled in Athens, Ontario.

He had one child, NOAH C., born in February, 1868, who married Minnie ———— and lives in Athens, Ontario.

3d. HELEN M., born November 3, 1836, married Martin Kinnie of Antwerp, February 18, 1858, had two children, and now lives in Hermon.

Her children are: 1st, BOWER, born about 1860, and died; 2d, FRANK, born April 19, 1865, married Maud Handcock December 30, 1892, and is settled in Hermon.

4th. HENRY C., born May 9, 1838, married Mary E. Green March 22, 1858, settled in Hermon, had five children, and died May 19, 1877, aged 39. His widow lives in the same town.

His children are: 1st, MARION, born July 14, 1859, married Wilbur N. Failing February 12, 1874, settled in Baltimore, and has two children, FRANCES, born June 14, 1879, and CHARLES C. W. H., born in December, 1891; 2d, IDELLE, born September 21, 1862, and lives in Hermon; 3d, FRED, born September 20, 1865, married Florence Stewart June 24, 1891, and settled in Athens, Ontario; 4th, WILLIE, born in 1872, and died next year; 5th, BOWER, born July 27, 1876, and lives in Richville.

5th. MARION, born October 15, 1840, and died April 5, 1859, aged 18.

6th. ELIZA, born January 9, 1842, and lives in Hermon, unmarried.

7th. FRANCES A., born·November 15, 1844, married Ephraim Jacobs of Spragueville, January 1, 1873. He dying in 1882, she married again, Hiram B. Keene of Keenes, October 31, 1883, and is now settled in Gouverneur, and has one child, FLORENCE M., born May 17, 1886.

Section Seventh. IRA—seventh child of Anna Williams—was born about 1810, married Sophrona Kennon of DeKalb, in 1831, settled in the same town on a farm, where he had eight children, and died in 1882, aged 72.

His children were as follows:

1st. JOHN, born in 1832, and died young.

2d. ELIZA, born in 1835, and died in infancy.

3d. SALLY, born in 1837, married Manton Spencer of DeKalb in 1855, settled in Allegan, Michigan, and has one child, CHARLES.

4th. MARIA, born in 1839, and died, unmarried, of consumption in 1862, aged 23.

5th. JAIRUS, born in 1841, married Martha Keeler in 1865, and is now settled in Montrose, South Dakota.

He had four children; 1st, FRANK, born in 1865, married Nellie Smith in 1891, and has one child, MALVINA; 2d, CHARLES, born in 1868, and died in 1885;

3d, PERLEY, born in 1872; 4th, IDA, born in 1874, both at home.

6th. HENRY, born in 1845, married Martha Halle-gas in 1870, settle I in his native town, and had one child, and died in 1877, aged 32.

His child LESTER, born in 1874, lives with his uncle Jairus in South Dakota.

7th. THOMAS, born in 1847, was drowned in 1862, aged 15.

8th. LUCY, born in 1849–50, for several years had the care of her father, then married Thomas Flight between 1890–92, and settled in Sterling, Connecticut.

Section Eighth. JULIA A.—eighth child of Anna Williams—was born about 1812, married King Richardson of DeKalb, settled in Hermon, had seven children, and died many years ago.

Her children:

Their names and history are not known, save the youngest, ORLO, who married and settled in Russel.

Section Ninth. RUSSEL—ninth child of Anna Williams—was born about 1814, married Jane Doran of DeKalb, settled first in Hermon, then later in Springfield, Illinois, had five children, and died in the same town some years ago.

His children:

Their names and history are not known, save ANNA and JOHN.

Section Tenth. SALLY—tenth child of Anna Williams – was born in 1816, married James Smith of

7

DeKalb in 1846, settled in the same town on a farm, had one child, since deceased, and is now living a widow.

Section Eleventh. WALTER — eleventh child of Anna Williams—was born June 22, 1819, married Annette Hosford of Russell December 3, 1843, settled on the old homestead, then in Russell, and last in Windom, Minnesota, had six children, and died August 21, 1891, aged 72.

His children were as follows:

1st. GEORGE, born January 4, 1845, served three years in the civil war, where he died July 30, 1864.

2d. JAMES E., born October 28, 1846, served two years in the late war, married Ida Mosier of Minnesota, June 20, 1876, settled in the same state, and has three children.

His children are: 1st, BURT, born in 1877; 2d, NELLIE, born in 1885; 3d, AULDIN, born in 1887, and since died.

3d. CYRENA, born April 22, 1849, married W. W. Zuel in Minnesota, in November, 1875, has two children, and is still living.

Her children are: 1st, ARCHIE, born in 1881; and 2d, GRACE, born in 1885.

4th. MARTENA, born April 22, 1849, (twin of former), married H. K. Buck of Russell April 5, 1868, has three children, and is still living.

Her children are: 1st, BURT, born in 1869; 2d, FRANK, born in 1872; 3d, LEROY, born in 1889, and deceased.

5th. HATTIE, E., born January 2, 1853, married Charles A. Matthews in Minnesota in December, 1877, has six children, and is still living.

Her children are: 1st, MABEL, born in 1877 and died in 1892; 2d, PLINEY, born in 1879; 3d, MAUD, born about 1882; 4th, BLANCH, born in 1884; 5th, LUELLA, born in 1889; 6th, unknown.

6th. DANIEL P., born July 16, 1858, and lives in Windom, unmarried.

Section Twelfth. HARRIET — twelfth child of Anna Williams — was born in 1820, married Russell Smith in 1841, settled in Russell, had one child, and is now living in Hermon.

Her child MARY, born in 1843, married Duane Allen of Russell.

CHAPTER VIII.

SALLY TANNER.

SALLY—sixth child of Thomas Tanner, Jr.—was born
probably about 1785, and died young, in childhood or
maidenhood, but of whom nothing is known, save the
common tradition that there was such a daughter.

CHAPTER IX.

LUCY TANNER WATERMAN,

LUCY—seventh and youngest child of Thomas Tanner of Cornwall—was born January 14, 1791, in New Lebanon, moved with her parents in 1793, to Cooperstown, where she received her early training and a limited education.

She married Timothy Waterman* of Pierstown, in 1809, and settled in the same place, on a farm, raised a family of four sons and seven daughters, and died there of erysipelas in May, 1855, aged 64.

Lucy was a member of the Presbyterian church of Cooperstown, a faithful wife and good mother.

The following is the outline history of her family:

Section First. HIRAM—oldest child of Lucy Waterman—was born September 15, 1810, in Pierstown, married Lucy M. Russell in 1831, settled in Western New York, and had one child. His wife dying in 1833 he married again her sister, Mary A. Russell, in 1842, lived in Cooperstown and then in Michigan, had one child, and his wife died in 1843. He married third, Sarah A. Miller of Rockford, in 1845, where he resided forty years, and died March 10, 1883, aged 72.

---

* Timothy was born September 18, 1785, and died October 19, 1853. He was of New England stock, but his immediate ancestors are not known. Several branches of the family have been written up, but not this one. There was a Simeon Waterman of Cooperstown, and his son Rensselaer.

His children were as follows:

1st. MELANTHUS R., born October 17, 1832. married Eliza Lamson in 1858, in New Milford, Illinois, and settled later in Marathon, Iowa, has eleven children, and is still living.

His children are: 1st, LIZZIE, born in 1859, married W. F. Couch September 18, 1881, and has three children, BERENEICE, HARRY, and JAY; 2d, HIRAM, born in January, 1861, married Mary E. Couch December 7, 1884, and has two children, WILBER and RUSSELL; 3d, HARRY, born in December, 1863, married Nora Coulson November 22,1891, and has no children; 4th, JENNIE, born in December, 1865, married N. D. Thompson April 27, 1884, and has three children, HOWELL, FRANK, and ETHEL, and settled near home; 5th. ERNEST, born in November, 1867, and unmarried; 6th, CLINTON, born in April,1869, and unmarried; 7th, BEAULAH, born in August, 1870, married F. E. Reymon January 21, 1891, and has one child, EARL, settled in his native town; 8th, GEORGE, born in January, 1873, and unmarried; 9th, ALICE, born in February, 1875, and married Ai Shaffer October 30, 1892; 10th, MAUDE, born in April, 1878, and unmarried; 11th, GARFIELD, born in September, 1881, and at home.

2d. MARY A., born February 1, 1843, married Charles M. Woolsey in 1867, settled in Rockford, Illinois, and has one child, GRACE MAY, and is still living.

Section Second. HARRIET—second child of Lucy Waterman—was born July 25, 1811, married Oliver N.

Drake of Cooperstown, December 21, 1831, settled in the same town, had five children, and died November 21, 1853, aged 42.

Her children were as follows:

1st, 2d, and **3d,** died in early childhood.

4th. GEORGE W., born in 1844, enlisted at 17 in the civil war, was in several battles, served to its close, and was promoted to first lieutenant. After the war he settled in New Orleans, and died in 1868, aged 24.

5th. OLIVER J., born in 1847, enlisted in the civil war when 14, and served to its close, married Alice J. Cobb October 10, 1878, settled in Rockford, and has no children.

Section Third. PHILANDER—third child of Lucy Waterman—was born March 20, 1813, married in 1838, settled in Pierstown, had one child, and buried his wife. He married again, went west, settled in DeKalb county, Illinois, on a farm, had four children, and died April 14, 1883, aged 70, leaving his widow and children who are supposed to be still living in the same town, but whose address and history are not known.

His children are as follows:

1st. ALICE, born August 10, 1844, raised and educated by her grandparents, married Volney M. Southgate in 1862, settled in Rockford, and has no children.

2d. BELLE.

3d. GEORGE.

4th. EMMA.

5th. DOUGLASS.

Section Fourth. ANN ELIZA—fourth child of Lucy Waterman—was born October 23, 1814, married Darius W. Pearsalls September 19, 1833, settled in Harpersville, New York, had one child, and died March 11, 1836.

Her child is:

ANN E., born October 29, 1835, married Oscar Dickenson November 14, 1855. He dying, she married again E. E. Lawton, June 18, 1867, and settled in Ninevah, New York, has no children, and is still living.

Section Fifth. CLARISSA — fifth child of Lucy Waterman—was born February 15, 1816, married Lewis N. Brainard * in Pierstown March 4, 1841, settled in Cooperstown, and had two children. In 1855 she moved to Sterling, Illinois, and there died, in September, 1879, aged 63.

Her children are as follows:

1st. ANNA E., born August 23, 1842, married Gordon M. Pierce, a soldier in the civil war, June 5, 1866, settled in Sterling, and her husband follows carpentering. She has no children.

2d. HARRIET, born June 4, 1844, married William Cavert of Washington county, Pennsylvania, a machinist, May 18, 1865, and is now settled in Denver, Colorado, but the history of the family is not further known.

Section Sixth. GEORGE — sixth child of Lucy Waterman—was born October 26, 1817, married Phœbe

---

* Lewis N., son of Icabod and Orpha Brainard, of Broome county, New York, was born January 12, 1812, followed the carpenter's trade, and died January 6, 1887, aged 75.

A. Millard of Ballston, New York, about 1841, and settled in Cooperstown, had two children, and died in April, 1871, aged 53.

His children are as follows:

1st. HENRY B., born May 18, 1842, educated at Yale college, studied law and theology in Chicago, and was ordained to the Baptist ministry in 1869. He married Auronetta Sherman August 21, 1877, settled in Chicago, and has two children.

His children are: EDITH, born November 12, 1878, and CLARA, born June 28, 1882.

2d. HARRIET, born in 1851, in Belvidere, married Robert Rowland, about 1870-3, settled in Rockford, and has no children.

Section Seventh. ALVIRA—seventh child of Lucy Waterman—was born May 5, 1819, never married, but lived and labored at her parents' home in Pierstown, and died January 11, 1855, aged 35.

Section Eighth. LUCY — eighth child of Lucy Waterman—was born April 12, 1823, married George Chaffee of Cooperstown March 23, 1851, settled in Belvidere, Illinois, in 1852, had one child, and died October 16, 1856, aged 33.

Her child was:

LILLIE R., born September 7, 1855, married E. J. Munn, a farmer. March 7, 1883, settled in her native town, and has no children.

Section Ninth. WILLIAM — ninth child of Lucy Waterman—was born October 2, 1826, married Anna W.

Warren November 20, 1855, and settled in Hyde Park, Illinois, has two children, and is still living, in 1892.

His children are as follows:

1st. ELLA W., born July 8, 1858, married (name not known) November 28, 1878, and now a widow with two children, WILLIAM and CLIFFORD.

2d. MAY S., born in 1860, and died in 1866.

Section Tenth. MARY ANN—tenth child of Lucy Waterman—was born March 1, 1830, married Oliver N. Drake about 1854-5, settled in Rockford, had no children, and died in October, 1889, aged 59.

Section Eleventh. EMILY—eleventh child of Lucy Waterman—was born July 16, 1832, married Owen Howard between 1856-8, settled later in Topeka, Kansas, had two children, and died there in January, 1879, aged 47.

Her children are as follows:

1st. HARRIET, born August 2, 1860, married George Armstrong in 1882, and settled in Kansas.

She has three children: 1st, LEE; 2d, WINNIE; 3d, FLOYD.

2d. HENRIETTA, born September 28, 1870, married Charles W. Allen, attorney, September 10, 1890, settled in Chicago, and has no children.

APPENDIX A.

THE GENEALOGY OF WILLIAM TANNER.

WILLIAM—son of Thomas and Martha Tanner—was born in Rhode Island, perhaps Newport, about 1725–30, moved with his parents in 1740 to Cornwall, Connecticut, married Hannah Newcomb of Kent, March 23, 1749, and settled in Cornwall. He had six children, the dates of whose birth and their names are in the Cornwall records. He was an active business man and farmer, and died young, about 1765.

His children were as follows:

I

Consider — born in June, 1750, married Rachel Benedict March 3, 1772, had ten children, and settled in Cornwall, but of whose life and death nothing is known.

His children were:

1st, HANNAH, born February 10, 1773.
2d, ASENATH, born January 11, 1775.
3d, WILLIAM, born February 7, 1777.
4th, BENJAMIN, born August 30, 1779.
5th, FREDRIC, born December 15, 1781.
6th, OLIVE, born November 18, 1784.
7th, EBENEZER, born March 4, 1788.
8th, RACHEL, born January 24, 1791.

9TH, SAMUEL, born January 12, 1794.

10TH, SYLVIA, born February 25, 1796.

Further than these data obtained from the Cornwall records, nothing is known of the history of these children, but it is believed that some of their descendants are living in Columbia and Hillsdale counties, New York.

II

Tryal — born December 20, 1751, married Huldah Jackson, probably daughter of Abram Jackson, of Cornwall, May 12, 1777, settled east and had four children, but his history is unknown.

His children were as follows:

1ST, PRIOR, born in February, 1788.

2D, PANTHEA, born in January, 1790.

3D, JULIUS, born in July, 1795.

4TH, BRIDGET, born in April, 1801.

Of their life and lineage nothing is known.

III

Ephraim — born June 4, 1754, married Huldah Munson of Vermont between 1775–80, settled in Warren, Connecticut, had eight children, and died in the same town in 1801, aged 47.

His children were as follows:

1ST, MARVIN, born about 1780, married Cornelia Tanner, his cousin, settled in Canaan, had four children, and died "many years ago," in the same town.

His children were: 1st, KATHARINE, who died young;

two others whose names are not known; 4th, CELIA, born between 1810–14, married Samuel Dewey, and lives in Los Angeles, California.

2D, CYRUS, born about 1785, married Lucy Sturtevant of Warren, Connecticut, settled in Illinois, had three children, and died " some years since."

His children were: 1st, LUCINDA, of whom nothing is known; 2d, MIRANDA, who married one Salter, and settled in Springfield. Illinois; 3d, WILLIAM, who died young.

3D, JOSEPH ALLEN, born in 1792, married Ora Swift of Cornwall in 1813, and had five children. In 1832 he moved to Waverly, Illinois, and died there in 1838. He was a Christian man, and deacon of the church.

His children were: 1st, ELISHA, born about 1814, married, and was drowned while crossing the Natches some years ago; 2d, HULDAH, born in 1816, married Augustine Curtis, and settled in Waverly, Illinois; 3d, SUSAN, born about 1818, and deceased; 4th, EPHRAIM, born between 1820–5, and deceased; 5th, EDWARD A., born between 1830–5, married Marion Brown of Waverly, January 25. 1861, and had two sons. He became a prominent minister and president of Illinois College, Jacksonville, and died in February, 1892. His sons were ALLAN A., and FREDDIE.

4TH, LYDIA, born between 1785–90, married Silas Beckley of Canaan, Connecticut, and is deceased.

5TH, LUCY, born about 1794, married Warren Sturtevant of Warren, Connecticut. had two or more children. and is dead.

Her children were: 1st, Christopher, secretary of the chamber of commerce, Minneapolis; 2d, another son, who has a son, the Rev. J. M. Sturtevant of Galesburg, Illinois.

6th, Patty, born about 1796, married Dr. Ralph Carter of Warren, Connecticut, had two children, and is dead.

Her children are: 1st, Lucy, who married one Weller, of Hartford; 2d, Cyrus, of Glastenburg, Connecticut.

7th, Lucinda, born in 1798, and died at 20 years, unmarried.

8th, Maranda, born in 1800, and died younger than her sister.

IV

Ebenezer — born January 20, 1757 and said to have been a soldier in the revolution, married Lydia Hatch February 20, 1782, settled in Warren, Connecticut, had eight or nine children of whom several died in infancy, and died in 1819, aged 62.

His other children were as follows:

1st, Ebenezer, born between 1783–5, married December 21, 1815, Dimmes Eldred of Warren, where he settled, had seven children, one dying in infancy, and died in April, 1862.

His children were: 1st, Thalia, born in 1817, married Henry Carter of Warren, November 13, 1845, had four sons and is still living, but her sons, save one, are all dead; 2d, William E., born in 1819, married Julia Foot April 12, 1849, had four children, and is now living in Winsted, Connecticut. His children are, MARVIN H., born in 1850, and is in business in Winstead, VICTOR, born in 1852, and died in 1870, LUCINDA, born in 1854, and died in 1866, and EGBERT WM., born in 1856, and now living in Winsted. 3d, LYDIA, born in 1821, married Harvey P. Hopkins of Warren, August 8, 1844, has five children, and is still living. Her children are EDWARD S., ELLA, ARTHUR, FRANK, and BURTON. 4th, LUCINDA, born in 1826, and died in 1848; 5th, ALMYRA, born in 1831, and died in 1858, both dying unmarried; 6th, SAMUEL E., born in 1833, married first Lucy A. Robinson January 5, 1867, and had two children. His wife dying he married second Hattie Smith, January 1, 1883. settled in Warren and has two more children; their names being CLARENCE, ARDEN, RAY, and HERBERT.

2D, HULDAH C., born August 1, 1793, married Aaron Sacket of Warren, May 15, 1816, moved to Ohio in 1840, had nine children, and died there in 1855. Her children were THEODOCIA, HARRIET, GEORGE, SARAH, EMELINE, WILLIAM, SETH, MARIA, and FRANCES. Their history is unknown.

3D, HARRIET, born April 1, 1795, married Erastus Curtis of Warren, January 14, 1819, had five children, and died March 28, 1837. Her children were CHARLES, FRANKLIN, ELLEN, DOWNS, and RALPH.

4TH, MALINDA, born May 2, 1797, married Charles Ambler of Bethlehem, January 21, 1835, had one child, and died June 4, 1842. Her child JOHN is living in Bristol, Connecticut.

V

William — born January 28, 1762, married ———,
had six children, is supposed to have settled in Hillsdale, Columbia county, New York, and died October
13, 1822.

His children were as follows:

1st, WILLIAM, JR., born in 1789, served in the war
of 1812, was in the battle of New Orleans, where he
died in January, 1815.

2D, RALPH, born in 1791, married Laura Pierson of
Long Island about 1818–20, settled in Madison county,
had four children, moved later to Cannon Falls, Minnesota, and died in March, 1868, aged 77.

His children were:

1st, WILLIAM P., born in December, 1821, married
Elizabeth Colville of Forestville, New York, in August,
1848, had five children, and died in 1883. His children
are, 1, WALTER, born in 1851, married Anna Pryor in
August, 1880, and had no children; 2, WILLIAM, born
in 1853, married Anna Krabiel in October, 1878, and
his children are WALTER, born in March, 1880, FLOR-
ENCE, born in January, 1882, WILLIAM P., born in
November, 1884, and HARRY C., born in October,
1887; 3, KATHARINE, born in 1856, is unmarried and
follows teaching in Cannon Falls; 4, GEORGE L., born
in 1858, married Carrie Cross in November, 1886, has
child, WILLIAM R., born in July, 1889, and is still
living; 5, MARY, born in 1862, and is unmarried.

2d, GILSON, born about 1823, and died young.

3d, HORACE ALLEN, born in Madison, New York,

September 28, 1830, married first Charlotte J. Barker of Homer, New York, second, Ellen B. Judge of Ireland, May 30, 1845, settled first in Cannon Falls, Minnesota, in 1856, second in Hastings, and then in DeLand, Florida, in 1881, and has six children. His children are 1, LAURA A., born in Hastings August 3, 1866, married W. A. Allen of DeLand, and has one child, CHARLES L.; 2, JOHN R., born in Hastings February 29, 1868; 3, MARY F., born in Hastings October 27, 1873; 4, LOUISE A., born in Hastings November 27, 1876; 5, WILLIAM J., born in Hastings November 3, 1878; 6, GEORGE A., born in same town March 28, 1880.

4th, ULYSSES born December 28, 1832, married Louise ———, and has no children.

3D, CLARA TANNER, born in 1793, married ——— Watson, of ———, and has two children.

Her children are: 1st, DELIA, born ———, unmarried, and residing in Washington, D. C.; 2d, JANE, born ———, married ——— Tucker, and settled in Solsville, New York.

4TH, MARCIA TANNER, born in 1795, married one Stuart of ———.

5TH, CORNELIA TANNER, born in 1797, married Marvin Tanner, her cousin, settled in Canaan, Connecticut, had four children, and long since died.

Her children are: 1st, KATHARINE, who died young, two others, names not known, and 4th, CELIA, who married Samuel Dewey of Los Angeles, California.

6TH, SALLY TANNER, born about 1800, married first one Rodman and then one Brown.

VI

Joseph Tanner — born in June, 1763, but of whose marriage, death, and descendants nothing is known.

APPENDIX B.

CORNWALL.

Cornwall, situated near the northwest corner of Connecticut in the county of Litchfield, is about nine miles long by six miles wide. It has the Hoosatonic river running along its western boundary, and two ranges of low mountains extending through the town north and south, in which are important mines of iron ore. The whole country is hilly and picturesque.

The town was first laid out in 1738, by the Fairfield Company into fifty-three "rights," or homesteads, of nearly a square mile each, and sold to early settlers. In 1740 the first permanent settlements were made by thirteen families, some of whose names were Jewet, Spaulding, Allen, Barret, Squires, Griffin, Roberts, and Fuller, followed soon after by several others, among them being Thomas and William Tanner, from Rhode Island, with their families. In 1741 the first minister, Rev. Solomon Palmer, a graduate of Yale college, settled in the town.

These settlements are supposed to have been made in the southern part where the first village of Cornwall was located; but soon after settlements were made in the north part, in Cornwall Hollow, lying among the mountains. Among these settlers was one William Tanner, Jr., called "Great Tanner," from his large

person, and to distinguish him from others of the same
name, who located on a farm since owned by Eber
Harrison. In the Hollow are at present a church,
school-house, saw-mill, and a few dwellings.

About the same time a settlement was made in the
south part on a high hill or eminence, by one Dudley,
and others, and called Dudleytown. Among these settlers was William Tanner, Sr., from Rhode Island.
Here quite a village sprang up, but there now remains
only two houses.

At present there are several other small centers as
East and West Cornwall.

Like most inland towns in those primitive times, the
growth of Cornwall was moderate. The work of clearing the lands of their heavy timber, of making roads, of
building up homes, of paying taxes, and securing a
scanty living was arduous and difficult. The markets
were poor and distant, and the accumulation of wealth
and comforts slow and limited.

We find the record of few incidents of those early
days, but here are one or two:

About 1755 William Tanner built a bridge over the
Hoosatonic between Cornwall and Sharon, near Abram
Jackson's farm, on private subscription, but which
failed to pay. In 1757 he petitioned the general court
for relief, which was granted by allowing him to levy
toll on the travel of the bridge. In 1761 this William
Tanner and Benoni Peck memorialized the court to set
up a lottery for the purpose of raising £300 with which
to clear the river of obstructions, and the court appoint-

ed five managers to sell tickets and raise the money, but the scheme, through mismanagement failed to accomplish its object.

During this early period, too, the French and Indian war broke out, and those who were able to bear arms were called into service, either to defend their own homes, or more distant points. Among them was Thomas Tanner, who enlisted at eighteen and served two years. And a few years after the close of this war difficulties arose with England about taxation, which soon developed into all the fears and excitements of a prospective war with "the mother country," and culminated a few years later in open hostilities.

In anticipation of this war the town of Cornwall in 1773 enlisted a "train band" or company for drill and any sudden emergencies. Of this company Thomas Tanner was appointed ensign by the general court, and two and a half years later was made second lieutenant of Captain Smith's company. Tradition says that one Ebenezer and a Loyal Tanner served in the same war.

Of the succeeding history of Cornwall for a hundred years we have no account, but there are records of births and marriages of Tanners there down to 1800; none, however, have lived in the town for many years. At the beginning of this century they began to migrate east and west, and their descendants are now found all over the country.

The population of the town in 1880 was 1,583, and in 1890 it was 1,283, of these the village contained 547.

showing a decrease of population during the last ten years.

Like many eastern towns, suffering from constant emigration of its people and business to more western regions, its progress has been slow, but the place is interesting for its history and traditions.

APPENDIX C.

NEW LEBANON.

New Lebanon is situated in Columbia county on the eastern border of New York, among the foot hills of the Hoosic mountains,—a wild, hilly, and romantic country. It derives its name from Lebanon, Connecticut, whence came the first settlers about the close of the revolution. Hither from Cornwall in 1781 came Thomas Tanner and his sons Ira, Thomas, Zera, and Isaac; also the sons of William Tanner, and several related families, besides settlers from other parts of New England, and occupying the country about the present village of New Lebanon.

Later, in 1787, the Shakers, originally from England, but more recently from near Albany, made settlements at Mount Lebanon, in the eastern part of the town. They established themselves in seven communities of fifty to one hundred persons each. A plain, honest, and industrious people they have followed as their principal occupation agriculture, horticulture, and broom manufacture. Though a singular order of society, they have been very peaceful and prosperous.

Still later the Thermal Springs of eastern Lebanon became celebrated, principally for their heavy flow of water at a temperature of seventy degrees, and for their medicinal propertie , having, however, the taste of pure

water. In more recent years they have become a
popular resort, have drawn about them a considerable
population of summer visitors, and are provided with
large hotels, parks, drives, and other attractions.

The village of New Lebanon, in and around which
were made the earliest settlements, has now a considerable population and business; a grist and saw-mills, two
machine shops, glass and vinegar factories, two news-
papers, good schools, a female seminary, and eight
churches, with fine streets, business blocks and
residences.

But our interest in the town is mainly confined to the
olden times, people, and history, where for a few years
resided our ancestors in their log cabins, subsisting
on coarse and scant fare, dressing in home-made linen
and woolen, having few privileges of education and
culture, enduring many deprivations and hardships, but
living in joyful hope of better times and richer
blessings.

While a few more remote relatives have continued to
dwell in this and surrounding towns, all our more direct
ancestors have long since removed and gone to their
long home.

A more complete history of the descendants of William
Tanner living in Columbia and Duchess counties is
greatly to be desired.

APPENDIX D.

COOPERSTOWN.

Cooperstown is beautifully situated at the foot of Otsego Lake, " the glimmer glass," and along the west shore of the outgoing Susquehanna, upon elevated ground sloping towards both the lake and river, and overlooked by mountains on the northeast. The town was early laid out in three long streets running north and south, and in six shorter streets running east and west, but has been much extended since. The first building erected was a blockhouse of hewn logs, fifteen feet square. In 1786 the first settlements were made by William Cooper, of Burlington, New Jersey, the proprietor of the town and large landholder; by Mrs. Johnson, who put up the first frame house; by White, Ellison, Guild, and several others. In the summer of 1787, more settlers, some from Connecticut, came in, who located in the village or took up adjacent land, and put up log tenements. The next year the village was platted, Mr. Cooper built his " Manor House," the "old Cooper mansion," and settlements became more rapid. In 1790 the village contained seven frame houses and some 50 people, with many more settlers in the surrounding country. The following year there were 20 houses and 100 inhabitants, the growth of the village being considerable for the time. This year Cooperstown was

made the county seat, a court house was built, R. R.
Smith established the first store, James Averell set up
the first tannery, and some one erected the first tavern,
"the Red Lion."

In 1792, and onward several more families came in,
among them Rensselaer and Richard Williams, merchants, Joshua Dewey, who taught the first school, succeeded by Oliver Corey, who taught many years. Dr.
Fuller commenced a long practice of medicine, and
many more emigrated into the outlying towns. But in
these primitive times the growth of the town was not
rapid, and we have no notes of interest till 1795, when
the first newspaper was set up, the " Otsego Herald,"
and the " Academy" was established containing three
rooms, in which Mr. Corey taught the school; and the
first religious meetings were held by Rev. Elisha Mosely,
though the first regular minister was Rev. Isaac Lewis,
who came in 1800.

At this time the village numbered about 200 inhabitants, some 35 families, and as many dwellings besides
public buildings. But surrounding towns settled equally
early were also springing up, as Pierstown, Fly Creek,
Plainfield, Richfield, Unadilla, Oneonta, now the largest
city in the county, and Cherry Valley, the oldest town,
having been settled in 1740.

From this time onward for 10 or 15 years, the growth
of Cooperstown was gradual but steady, depending upon
the trade of the country, upon local demand for manufactures, and upon county business. The growth was
necessarily slow, for the country was mostly cov-

ered with heavy forests, the people were poor, many lived in log cabins, and trade was very limited.

In 1812 there were in Cooperstown 183 houses, 686 inhabitants, and in 1820 about 1000 residents beside the outlying population. The town has been growing slowly ever since that period and at present is one of the most beautiful county seats and pleasant summer resorts in the state, having a population of about 3,000.

This village and the country about, early became the residence of many of our ancestors. Here Ira and Thomas Tanner settled about 1790, and two or three years later came their parents and with them their four brothers and sisters, Zera, Isaac, Anna and Lucy, who made homes in the village or adjacent country. With them came others, who later married into the Tanner families—viz., Waterman, Fitch, Williams, Dewey, Stacy, Stewart and Westcott. All these families became familiar with the scenes and persons described above, and they all experienced the deprivations and hardships of early pioneer life.

APPENDIX E.

DE KALB.

The township of DeKalb,—the name being derived from Baron DeKalb,—is situated in Northern New York in St. Lawrence county, about twenty miles from Ogdensburg and forty from Watertown, and was originally ten miles square, but has since been reduced in size.

The country is broken, hilly, and rocky, having many outcropping ridges of granite and limestone, with occasional veins of iron ore and other minerals. It was primarily covered with beech, maple, some hemlock, pine, and other timber. The streams all trend toward the St. Lawrence river, giving the land a northern slope. The climate is cold, not adapted to fruit and grains, though natural to grass and grazing.

This town, with others, was originally purchased by Alexander Macomb, who sold it to Samuel Ogden, native of New Jersey, who resold the town in 1803 to Judge William Cooper. He, the same year, accompanied a colony of thirty-four persons from Cooperstown and Richfield across the country to his new purchase. After some severe experiences along the way they arrived in June with their teams and goods and began a settlement on the Oswegatchie just above Cooper's Falls, since known as "Old DeKalb." Among the party were Rich, Stacy, Merrill, Cook, Brown, Stone,

Ransom, Utley, Wright, McCullam, Farr, Bell, Campbell, Woodhouse, Stockwell, Dimick, Hewlett, and Sloan. The first two days two log cabins were put up and covered with bark, and the third day a log store was erected to receive the supplies and goods sent in by the judge.

That season several farms were surveyed and clearings begun. The next spring the *families* of several of the above came in; also James Cooper and his sons, Haskins, Dodge, Dr. Seeley, Barton, the Alexanders, Pooler, Burnett, Holt, Colonel Griffin, Goff, who surveyed and mapped the town, and the family of Isaac Stacy, the first supervisor.

This same year the first settlement was made at Richville by Soloman Rich and Jonathan Haskins. Here soon quite a village sprang up, Soloman Pratt keeping the first hotel in 1807, and Joseph Kneeland the first school. Still later, stores and mills were erected and churches organized.

In the autumn of 1804 a violent rain of several days flooded the valley of the Oswegatchie, and caused the death of one person, much damage to property and inconvenience to the people.

In 1805 more settlers came in, among them Benedict, Preston, Johnson, Smith and his six sons, Cleghorn, and Soloman Pratt. This year Judge Cooper built his hotel, sixty feet square and three stories high; also a grist-mill at the falls. Marriages and births as usual began to take place.

In the spring of 1806 the town was organized and a

town meeting held. The next winter the first school
was taught by Bela Wills, a Methodist minister, who
held the first religious meetings and formed the first
church in town.

In the spring of 1809, the first settlement was made
at East DeKalb by several related families from Cooperstown, who came across the country with their teams,
stock, and goods. They were Thomas Tanner, Isaac
Tanner, John Williams, and Joshua Dewey, with their
families; also Philemon Stewart and wife, one Adams,
and John Westcott. These settled at the "Corners" or
on surrounding farms.

Here soon a school was opened, and in 1817 a Presbyterian church organized under the labors of Rev. James
Johnson. This church consisted of Thomas and Anna
Tanner, of Deacon Pomeroy and wife, and Deacon
Burnett and wife, of John and Anna Williams, and
Isaac and Nancy Burnham, and some others. Several
powerful revivals of religion were enjoyed, a house of
worship was erected out of the native sandstone and
granite, and the church long prospered. But the old
members dying or removing, and few of the next generation succeeding them, the church has now become
extinct, and the house of worship has crumbled to
ruins.

East DeKalb has never become a permanent center of
business, surrounding towns supplying the wants of the
people. The old pioneer families and Tanner relatives
have all disappeared, and a generation that "knew not
Joseph" has taken their places.

The main agricultural interests have always been stock raising, and prominently dairying, but these interests are not as prosperous as formerly.

Owing to the reduced productiveness of the soil and the removal of the younger generation west, the growth of the town in population and wealth has been slow.

APPENDIX F.

WARSAW.

The town of Warsaw, situated near the center of Wyoming county, was originally a part of the " Holland Purchase," which included several counties of western New York. It lies forty-two miles southwest of Rochester and forty-five miles southeast of Buffalo, on the old stage line running to the latter city. It is thirteen miles southeast of Attica.

Warsaw is centrally divided north and south by the Oatka, its surface gently sloping from the east and west to the central valley. The first actual purchase of land and settlement in the town were made by Elihu Webster in 1803, who took up a large track of over 3,000 acres, some being located in the central valley and most of which he soon resold. While the surrounding lands were early taken up and settlements begun, yet for several years little progress was made in settling and building up the village. The first saw mill was built in 1804, and a grist mill a year or two later. About this time the first school house was built and school taught by Samuel McWhorter. Also a store erected and tavern established.

Very early religious meetings were held and in 1808 the first Presbyterian church was organized, but not till 1828 was the first newspaper issued. The growth of the town was slow until 1816, when several new buildings were erected and business began to develop, on a small scale, however. Under the primitive conditions then existing this could not be otherwise, for the country being heavily timbered with beech and maple, the work of clearing was slow and expensive. The new settlers, being mostly poor, had a hard struggle to pay for their land, to meet their taxes, and to obtain a coarse and scanty living.

But the opening of the Erie Canal in 1825 along their northern border brought relief, afforded a better market for their home produce and a cheaper portage for their merchandise.

The location of the county seat here in 1840 gave another impetus to growth, building, and business, and later, in 1852, the running of the Erie railroad through the town afforded still better markets and cheaper transport.

Still later extensive salt works were built, and a sanitarium with salt baths established. The country grew in wealth and intelligence, schools and churches multiplied and improved, trade and manufactures increased, until the village has become wealthy and beautiful, a place of 4,000 inhabitants.

But our interest is connected more especially with the early struggles and growth of the town, with the primitive history of its settlers, upon whom fell the heavy work of clearing away the forests, building roads, and laying the foundations of educational and Christian institutions, and securing the comforts and blessings of

9

civilized life. For among these pioneers were our own relatives and the families with whom they intermarried.

They were the elder Zera Tanner and his growing family, the Websters, McWhorters, Fosters, Woods, Spencers, and others with their families. These all shared in the struggles with primitive surroundings, in the severe labor of clearing· up farms and building homes, in the hardships of poor markets and plain and insufficient living, and in the ambitions and hopes of improving their condition and of seeing better times.

But some of them died young, fell before the destroyer in the midst of their toils without realizing their expectations. Only their children entered into the fruits of their labors and enjoyed the blessings so dearly purchased; but even most of them have gone hence, and a generation has come forward that knows neither the fathers and their toils, nor the source and cost of their pleasant surroundings and many comforts.

[THE END.]

www.ingramcontent.com/pod-product-compliance
Lightning Source LLC
Chambersburg PA
CBHW030613270326
41927CB00007B/1155

* 9 7 8 3 3 3 7 1 0 1 8 0 0 *